# PATHS OF T

John Blakesley was born ... Chester. He studied theolo... training for the priesthood ... served curacies at Egremont in Cumbria, and in Doncaster. In 1979 he became Vicar of St Helen Auckland in Co. Durham, a parish containing two former mining villages near Bishop Auckland. He also lectures on liturgy at Durham University.

# PATHS
# OF THE HEART

*Prayers of Medieval Christians*

JOHN BLAKESLEY

First published 1993
Triangle
SPCK
Holy Trinity Church
Marylebone Road
London NW1 4DU

*British Library Cataloguing in Publication Data*
A catalogue record for this book is available from the British Library.
ISBN 0–281–04663–8

Typeset by Inforum, Rowlands Castle, Hants
Printed in Great Britain by
BPCC Hazell Books
Aylesbury, Bucks
Member of BPCC Ltd

# Contents

## THE CHRISTIAN DAY      *1*

Morning hymn — Christ the dayspring — God's
presence — Remembering the cross — Evening hymn
— Christ our peace — Prayers for God's protection —
Alcuin's prayer in the night

## THE EUCHARIST      *13*

Preparation for Communion — Prayer before receiving
Communion — Meditation on the sacrament —
O sacred banquet — After Communion — Self-offering

## THE CHRISTIAN YEAR      *21*

Advent — Christmas — Circumcision of Christ —
Epiphany — Ash Wednesday — Passiontide: the cross,
Christ's wounds, the last words — Palm Sunday —
Maundy Thursday — Good Friday, Mary at the cross —
Holy Saturday — Easter morning, Mary Magdalen in
the garden — The Good Shepherd — Ascension Day —
Pentecost — Trinity Sunday — Feast of the
Transfiguration — Holy Cross Day

## PERSONAL DEVOTION      *51*

Praise for earth and heaven — Our redemption — God's
mercy — Longing for God — Guidance in doubt —
Honest anger — Christ's incarnation — The elusive

Lover — Christ's glory and humility — Love of Christ
— Fountain of mercy — Heavenly Jerusalem — Our
need of God — Christ the Good Shepherd — Christ the
High Priest — Growing in Christ — Praising the
Creator

## THE SAINTS

Mary: conception, nativity, annunciation, purification,
assumption — Benedict — John the Baptist — Mary
Magdalen — Michael and All Angels — Andrew —
Stephen — John the Apostle — Holy Innocents — All
Saints — Apostles — Martyrs

## INTERCESSION

Asking for the grace of love — Peace in the Church —
Reconciliation — For a bishop — Relatives —
Travellers — Blessing a house — For a pregnant woman
— The sick — The dead

# Foreword

The title of this book of medieval prayers by John Blakesley comes from a prayer of Berengar of Tours (d. 1088) which displays honest anger before God. There is great risk in opening one's heart honestly, with all its longings and hopes, its fears and vulnerabilities. Tremendous joy wells up and honest anger is exposed and in this way the structures of one's being are necessarily transformed. That is the reason why this collection of medieval prayers is so refreshing to ponder in quiet reflection, or to use in your own devotions. They contain joy and sorrow, love and anger, personal vulnerability and concern for others — all undergirded with a profound faith in the mercy and grace of God.

The devotion seen in these translations reaches back beyond the Reformation. It displays a warm, evangelical sense of personal love for God in Christ while at the same time bearing a strong catholic sense of the wholeness of the Church and a clear witness to the powerful doctrines of the Faith which are basic to both these traditions.

In the first section John Blakesley provides perceptive new translations of some familiar hymns and prayers through the day. These reveal the way in which the medieval Christian linked the progress of the hours with the providential mercy of God. I have been using this section lately in my own devotions. There is a beautifully Franciscan feel to the midday prayer which focuses on the Christ who at noontide shed his blood on the cross for the world's redemption.

The eucharistic prayers preserve some of the classic words of Thomas Aquinas the Dominican and Bonaventure the Franciscan. They affirm the presence of Christ in the sacrament and speak of the eucharist as a foretaste of heaven. They express the emotional and affective response of the believer, whose wounds of sin are healed by the healing wounds of Calvary, and for whom the sacrament is the bread of life and the medicine of immortality.

The strong liturgical sense of the medieval mind is linked

vii

with the personal and corporate sense of the believer in the section on the Christian year. The Advent prayers speak of the 'coming' of Christ in the words of the Gospel and in the consecration of the gifts in communion, relating these to the coming of Christ in humility in his incarnation and in glory at the consummation of all things.

The prayers of Lent and Passion are not sombre or depressing but point to the cross as the Tree of Life bearing the flowers and fruit of glory, as a ladder to heaven and as a beacon-light sending out its rays to dispel the darkness of the world's sin.

There is a lovely translation of Peter Abelard's Good Friday hymn which not only reveals the tenderness and sensitivity wrought in him by his tragic love-affair with Héloïse but also holds in healthy tension the objective value of the atoning work of Christ as well as its subjective application to the believer's heart.

We stand sharing the sorrow of Mary's heart at the foot of the cross and sound the depth of feeling in these medieval prayers of Holy Week. Yet we do not stay there, but are swept up into the Easter glory in a variety of strong biblical images in a rhythmic excitement by which the Resurrection is celebrated and experienced.

The section on personal devotion contains a mixture of godly sorrow and yearning for God, together with delight in salvation and tender expressions of mystical love for Christ. At one moment you are thirsting for God like the deer of the forty-second psalm and at the next you are searching for the lost coin like the woman in the Gospel parable. There is a prayer for guidance as to whether a proferred bishopric should be accepted and then the reader identifies himself or herself with Mary Magdalene in her experiences of forgiveness and adoring love at the feet of Christ. These are personal prayers of lively imagination, devotional depth and rapturous praise.

The section on the saints links the sometimes lonely path of the pilgrim with the communion of saints, beginning with Mary the chief of saints and drawing inspiration and example from apostles, martyrs and the angelic throng, not forgetting the simple but powerful witness of the Holy Innocents killed by Herod. Throughout this section there is rejoicing in suffering with the sure hope of ultimate joy in heaven in the presence and glory of Christ the King of Saints.

The final section contains prayers of intercession. Nothing is exempted from the merciful gaze of God and prayers are made in times of pregnancy, birth, life and death, for nothing falls outside his love.

In this multi-coloured tapestry of medieval prayers John Blakesley shows the reader the lights and shadows of human life within the love of God. Here is unfolded a rich texture of an underlying pattern of hope and trust which clings to God despite plague and adversity, sickness and poverty, and which affirms his love in this world and in the world to come.

The author's liturgical, historical and theological awareness pervades this collection of medieval prayers, yet he communicates the simplicity of the believing heart in the context of the divine Love.

*Brother Ramon* SSF
*The Society of St Francis*

## Acknowledgements

I should like to thank the following for their help and encouragement: my neighbour, the Revd Nicholas Beddow, for the initial suggestion for the book and for his experienced advice; Valerie Appleton for her beautifully accurate typing; my wife, Christine, for keeping me from living entirely in the Middle Ages; my daughters, Rosanna, Marion and Helen — the title was Helen's idea and Marion found the cover picture; my parents; and Wynne Raine, who, having traversed some very rough paths herself, has helped me on my journey.

# Introduction

Those who travel northwards through Yorkshire along the A1 are following for most of the way the line of the Roman road which the Saxons called 'Dere Street'. After Scotch Corner the road becomes a motorway and takes a newer and more easterly route, but the Roman line is continued into County Durham by a very straight B-road. On reaching the boundary of my parish, this degenerates into a country lane, then into an overgrown footpath, which plunges straight down a steep sandstone ridge along the edge of an ancient oak wood.

This footpath is one of my favourite walks, especially at dusk, when the partridges and lapwings are gathering in the fields before roosting, and the owls, ready for a night's hunting, are calling to each other in the wood. This part of the Roman road is mainly travelled by rabbits, foxes and badgers, as it must have been in Saxon times: 'Dere Street' means 'Animal Street', the paved road frequented by wild animals.

As well as being a delightful place to walk, this largely abandoned thoroughfare has come to symbolize for me that part of Christian history known as the Middle Ages. (Walking under the green canopy on a summer evening, one could almost *be* in the Middle Ages: one half expects to see Robin Hood appearing among the oak trees in the misty twilight!) By contrast the speeding traffic of the A1 a few miles to the south represents our late twentieth-century busyness in a world that has largely turned its back on medieval religion and dismissed it as riddled with ignorance, fear and superstition. Certainly there was a good deal of pathological religion around in medieval times, just as there is in any age, but there was also much wisdom, beauty and richness. In our own day, some of these riches are being rediscovered. Despite the great cultural divide of the Enlightenment, Hildegard of Bingen from the twelfth century and Julian of Norwich from the fourteenth have caught the imagination of many people, who find that their writings speak to them of God in a remarkably vivid and encouraging way.

We need our motorways (in the absence of a proper rail system!) and our purposive activity, but our lives are impoverished if we never take time to dawdle along the forgotten byways. They are hopeless as a means of rapid transit, but priceless as a source of delight and wonder; they allow us to enjoy the richness of life around us, to browse on beauty and to sense our continuity with the past.

We used to be told that 'prayer is work'. That may be true, but it seems to me still more true that prayer is play. It is a recreational activity, like a country walk, done for its own sake and not in order to achieve a particular objective. There are valuable spin-offs, of course. When children play, they are learning and growing through the activity all the time (as are we when we pray); but they don't do it for self-improvement — if they did, it would immediately cease being play — they do it because it's fun.

The most helpful definition of prayer that I have heard came from Fr Mark Gibbard, ssje, who said: 'Prayer is not so much asking; prayer is loving, or rather, being loved.' Using the language of popular psychology, one might go on to say that prayer is 'quality time' spent with a beloved person. With human beings, 'quality time' can be spent working together on a practical project, but it is usually spent doing something recreational: a drink, a meal, an outing, or making love. What matters is not so much the nature of the shared activity as just being with the loved one.

So it is too in the case of our 'quality time' with God. Whatever helps us to focus on the presence of the beloved and make his love for us a reality is a precious resource. We have, of course, the primary resources of the Bible, the sacraments and our fellow Christians. Then there are the ways in which God discloses to us his loving and life-giving presence in his creation: for example, through the beauties of nature, or art, or music. These, we may feel, are more than enough, but many people find still further resources for enriching their 'quality time' with God in the writings of Christians of past ages.

These prayers offer us a glimpse of how Christians in the Middle Ages took the images of God which came to them from Scripture and the tradition of the Church, and made them part of their own living relationship with him. Some of the prayers are also poems. This is no accident, because poetry and prayer both use language rich in imagery as they struggle to express things which cannot be stated literally.

In translating these pieces from their original Latin, I have often been struck by the freedom and playfulness with which their authors treated biblical images. Though well aware of their original context and meaning, these medieval Christians were not afraid to play around with the images and adapt them to suit their own needs, and we may find that some of the prayers will encourage us to do the same.

Like the images in dreams, poetic images and the enacted symbols of the liturgy have many layers of meaning. These layers are constantly being added to as each reader or worshipper approaches the poem or sacrament conditioned by experiences that are uniquely their own. Because prayer is play, we can allow ourselves to be dreamy, playful and imaginative in our thinking about God. We are not sitting an examination, we are spending time with our most beloved friend; we can afford to relax and be ourselves. Like the author of 'Christ the Good Shepherd' (p.68), we can let ourselves follow our association of ideas without feeling that we are being culpably distracted. That, after all, is how conversation goes between friends: one thing leads to another; it proceeds by chance association, not by pre-planned agenda.

We may, if we wish, let our imagination follow the paths taken by these medieval Christians and see what connections there are with our path through life today. In his soliloquy on Psalm 42 (p.57), for instance, the Venerable Bede takes the image of the thirsty deer and uses it to express his own longing for God, clothing the image with his personal language of love. We can think Bede's thoughts after him and then go on to add our own language of love and longing. Or we may prefer, having overheard these Christians at prayer, to strike out along paths of our own. As an example of what could happen, I find that my imagination embroiders the text 'Cast your burden upon the Lord' with the picture of someone meeting me at a railway station. I shrug from my shoulders a heavy rucksack containing a lot of pain, fear and anxiety. I hand it over, remembering the words 'Unload all your worries on to him, since he is looking after you.'

These translations are an attempt to beat down some of the forbidding brambles and nettles that have obscured these largely forgotten paths of Christian experience, so that their hidden riches may be more accessible. Notes accompany each text, and there are references to sources and more historical notes at the end of the book. I hope this collection will encourage some enjoyable wandering along the paths taken by medieval Christians as they communed with God in their hearts. May the words and images which nourished their relationship with God be enriching and life-giving to others.

*John Blakesley*
*St Helen Auckland, 1992*

# THE
# CHRISTIAN
# DAY

Morning hymn — Christ the dayspring —
God's presence — Remembering the cross —
Evening hymn — Christ our peace —
Prayers for God's protection —
Alcuin's prayer in the night

*My tongue will speak of your righteousness
and of your praises all day long.*
Psalm 35.28 (NIV)

## Morning hymn

Shadows of gloomy night are now retreating,
dawn brings the daylight, radiant and gleaming,
with all our being let us seek our maker,
    God the almighty.

Hear us, O Father, in your loving kindness,
drive from our spirits weariness and weakness,
grant us on earth and in your heavenly kingdom
    health and salvation.

Trinity blessed, Deity co-equal,
Father almighty, Son and Holy Spirit,
all earth resounds with echoes of your splendour;
    great is your glory.

This hymn, written before the eleventh century, was sung by the monks at their early morning service of Lauds. Perhaps it helped wake up the bleary-eyed among them by reminding them of the beauties of a new day.

## Christ the dayspring

Blessed and glorious are you, O Christ;
you have come to my heart,
Dayspring from on high.

Fountain of eternal love,
how can I forget you?
You graciously remember me
and give yourself to me.

You have dealt so lovingly with me your servant,
and have shown me such favour and friendship —
more than I could hope for, and more than I deserve.
How can I repay such graciousness?

Most kind Jesus,
grant that your grace may be with me,
and work with me,
and stay with me to the end.
Grant that I may always want and desire
whatever is most acceptable and pleasing to you.

The anonymous author of this prayer takes the image of the
dayspring from the song of Zechariah, the morning canticle *Benedictus* (Luke 1.67–79), where Christ is compared to the rising sun,
bringing light and warmth to the world.

## Early morning

In the first hour of this new day
may your mercy surround us, Lord:
that throughout the day we may be glad,
and find our delight in praising you.
Through our Lord Jesus Christ your Son,
who lives and reigns with you and the Holy Spirit,
one God for ever and ever.

This is a prayer from the office of Prime. The offices or 'hours'
provided the structure for the monastic day. They were services
consisting mainly of psalms and readings, and St Benedict (c.480–
c.550, the father of western monasticism) called them the *opus Dei*,
the 'work of God'. The prayer and praise they expressed was the
main work of the monk or nun.

## *Morning: God's presence*

Come, O Lord, and visit us in peace,
that we may rejoice in your presence
in sincerity of heart.


Waken our hearts, Lord,
to prepare the ways of your Son:
by his coming to us
may we be worthy to serve you
with a clear and fresh mind.

Although these were originally Advent prayers, they are suitable for
use in the morning, especially perhaps for those who, on waking up,
feel like Charles Wesley when he wrote:

Dark and cheerless is the morn
unaccompanied by Thee.

Even when morning brings the grey emptiness of grief or loneliness,
it also brings the chance to realize that we are in the company of a
friend who loves us more than we can imagine and in whose presence we can find joy again.

## *Midday: remembering the cross*

Lord Jesus Christ,
who at the sixth hour of the day
mounted the scaffold of the cross
for the redemption of the world,
and poured out your precious blood
for the forgiveness of our sins;
we humbly pray
that, being saved by your passion and your wounds,
we may be worthy after our death
to go in rejoicing through the gates of paradise.

During the later Middle Ages, especially under the influence of the Franciscans, devotion to the passion of Christ became extremely popular. This was the age of large crucifixes in churches, of Masses of the Holy Cross said on Fridays at special altars on top of the rood screen immediately below the cross, and of devotions which focused on particular physical aspects of the passion such as the five wounds or the crown of thorns. Midday, the hour of the crucifixion, was a natural time for them.

## Evening hymn

O God, creator of us all
and King of all the heavenly realms,
you clothe the day with beauteous light,
the night you grace with quiet sleep.

May weary bodies find through rest
the strength to take up work again;
let minds worn down with grief and care
obtain refreshment and relief.

So, when the night's deep shadows fall
and bring the daylight to a close,
our faith may still shine on undimmed
and turn the darkness into light.

Christ and the Father we adore,
and you, blest Spirit, with them one,
working through all things mightily:
cherish us, Holy Trinity.

This hymn was written by ST AMBROSE (d.397) who was Bishop of Milan and introduced hymns into the western Church. His course of instruction for baptism candidates still survives and is very informative about worship in the fourth century. He was a great influence on St Augustine, who, in his *Confessions* (ix.12), quotes the first two verses of this hymn to illustrate how sleep helped to alleviate his grief after the death of his mother St Monica.

### Night prayer: Christ our peace

Above all the things I desire,
grant to me, Lord, that I may rest in you,
and that my heart may find its peace in you.

You are the true peace of my heart,
you alone are its rest;
without you I am burdened with anxiety
that is hard to bear.

In this peace, then,
that is, in you who are my one supreme and eternal good
I will sleep and take my rest.

The author ends his prayer by echoing one of the psalms from Compline, Psalm 4.9 (BCP):

I will lay me down in peace, and take my rest:
for it is thou, Lord, only that makest me dwell in safety.

## *Prayers for God's protection*

Keep us safe, Lord, while we are awake,
and watch over us while we are asleep:
that awake we may be with Christ,
and asleep we may rest in peace.


We ask you, Lord, to visit this home,
and drive far from it all that is evil:
may your holy angels who dwell here keep us in peace,
and let your blessing be always upon us.
Through our Lord Jesus Christ your Son,
who lives and reigns with you and the Holy Spirit,
one God for ever and ever.

These prayers come from the office of Compline, which has been
the final service of the day in religious communities since the sixth
century.

## Alcuin's prayer in the night

He who slept calmly in the boat's stern,
then, rising, commanded the winds and the sea;
may he grant that, though my limbs rest here,
tired after hard work, my heart may be awake to him.
   Gentle Lamb of God,
    you have taken away all the world's sin.
   Keep me safe, while I rest,
    from all that may hurt me.

ALCUIN (*c*.735–804), the highly educated cultural adviser to the Emperor Charlemagne, reveals in this prayer a simple faith in God's love and power in a familiar situation of human vulnerability: the experience of being awake at night and feeling fear. Whether the things we are afraid of are burglars, or our own self-denigrating thoughts, or the prospect of facing the demands of tomorrow, we can afford to relax, like Jesus in the boat (Mark 4.38), and trust in God's love.

# THE
# EUCHARIST

Preparation for Communion — Prayer before
receiving Communion — Meditation on the
sacrament — O sacred banquet —
After Communion — Self-offering

*Whenever you eat this bread and drink this
cup, you proclaim the Lord's death until he comes.*
1 Corinthians 11.26 (NIV)

## *Preparation for Communion*

Most gentle God,
grant that as I receive the body of your Son
our Lord Jesus Christ,
which he took from his mother Mary,
I may be made fit to be incorporated into his mystical body
and to be numbered among his members.

Most loving Father,
grant that as I in my earthly pilgrimage
receive your beloved Son beneath a veil,
so I may finally gaze upon him face to face for ever;
who lives and reigns with you
in the unity of the Holy Spirit,
one God, world without end.

A prayer attributed to ST THOMAS AQUINAS (*c.*1225–74) the
great Dominican theologian. He was much influenced by the newly
rediscovered philosophy of Aristotle and his work has formed the
basis for most of Roman Catholic theology. He was also an accom-
plished poet: his image of the veil as a way of suggesting how Christ
is present in the sacrament occurs again in the poem on page 17.
'Incorporation' is another favourite (and biblical) idea of his: in receiving Communion the Christian is united not just with Christ,
but also with the other members of his mystical body, the Church.

*Prayer before receiving Communion*

O God our Father,
source and fountain of all goodness,
who, prompted by your mercy,
willed that your only Son
should come down to this world for our sake,
and take that flesh
which I, though unworthy, hold here in my hands;
I adore you,
I glorify you,
I praise you with all my heart.
And I pray that you will not abandon your servant,
but will forgive my sins,
so that I and all your people may be able to serve you
    alone,
the living and true God,
in purity of heart and body.
Through the same Christ our Lord.

From an English manuscript Mass-book, *c.*1320.

# Meditation on the sacrament

You I love devoutly, hidden truth divine,
lying truly hidden in this bread and wine:
all my heart's devotion now I give you here,
lost in contemplation of your presence dear.

Sight and taste and touching all are here deceived;
but the sense of hearing still can be believed.
I believe whatever God's own Son did say,
when truth's Word incarnate gave himself that day.

On the cross was hidden his divinity;
here concealed is also his humanity.
Both these I acknowledge with my firm belief,
and I seek his mercy, like the dying thief.

Though your wounds, like Thomas, I do not perceive,
yet my God is present — that I do believe.
May my faith in you grow ever more and more,
and my hope be in you — you whom I adore.

Jesus, now I see you veiled in hidden guise;
when shall I be given that most longed-for prize,
when shall I behold you, see you face to face,
in the blessed vision of your glorious grace?

A poem by ST THOMAS AQUINAS (see notes to p. 15). C.S. Lewis refers to this poem in his famous sermon 'The Weight of Glory', pointing out that we can meet Christ in one another as well as in the sacraments: 'Next to the Blessed Sacrament Itself your neighbour is the holiest object presented to your senses . . . in him also Christ . . . the glorifier and the glorified . . . is truly hidden.' (From *Transposition and Other Addresses* (Bles 1949).)

## *At Communion: O sacred banquet*

O sacred banquet,
in which Christ is received,
the memory of his passion is renewed;
our minds are filled with his grace,
giving us a pledge of the glory to come.
Alleluia,
Alleluia.

Grant, Lord, that in the life to come
we may ever rejoice in your divine life,
of which on earth we have a foretaste
as we receive your precious body and blood.

By ST THOMAS AQUINAS (see pp. 15 and 17).

*After Communion*

Dearest Lord Jesus,
pierce the very marrow of my soul
with the most sweet and healing wound of your love,
with true, peaceful, apostolic and most holy charity,
that my soul may languish and melt
with love and desire for you alone.
May it have a desire and longing to enter your courts,
may it yearn to be free and to be with you.
Let my heart always hunger for you,
and feed on you, whom angels delight to look upon;
let it always thirst for you, who are the fountain of life,
the source of wisdom, knowledge and eternal light,
the torrent of pleasure,
and the fertile abundance of the house of God.

A prayer attributed to ST BONAVENTURE (1221–74), a disciple of St Francis of Assisi. Though reserved English temperaments may shrink from such language, the author is certainly not afraid of emotionalism in prayer, nor of using erotic imagery to express his love for Christ. In this he is the heir of the anonymous eleventh-century author of the poem on p. 61 and of St Bernard of Clairvaux (see p. 62).

## *Self-offering*

Lord, take to yourself all my freedom:
take my memories,
my thoughts,
my plans
and my desires.
Whatever I have or possess, you have given me.
I give it all back to you,
and entrust it to the guidance of your will.
Only give me your love and your grace
and I am rich enough:
I ask for nothing more.

In the Eucharist we have the opportunity to entrust to God our deepest selves, including the bits of us that are vulnerable — memories, perhaps, which cause us pain, or desires that we're not proud of. In his love, God accepts the whole of us just as we are, without waiting for us to be 'good' (see also p. 56). Because we can always rely on God's love and grace, we can trust him to give us (whether in time or eternity) all the things which will make for our true flourishing and deep joy.

# THE
# CHRISTIAN
# YEAR

Advent — Christmas — Circumcision of
Christ — Epiphany — Ash Wednesday —
Passiontide: the cross, Christ's wounds, the
last words — Palm Sunday — Maundy
Thursday — Good Friday, Mary at the cross —
Holy Saturday — Easter morning, Mary
Magdalen in the garden — the Good Shepherd
— Ascension Day — Pentecost —
Trinity Sunday — Feast of the Transfiguration
— Holy Cross Day

*For God so loved the world that he gave his
one and only Son, that whoever believes in
him shall not perish but have eternal life.*

John 3.16 (NIV)

# *Advent*

You are our eternal salvation,
the unfailing life of the world.
Light everlasting,
you are truly our redemption.

Grieving that the human race was perishing
through the tempter's power,
without leaving the heights
you came to the depths in your loving kindness.

Readily taking our humanity by your own gracious will,
you saved all earthly creatures, long since lost,
restoring joy to the world.

Redeem our souls and bodies, O Christ,
and so possess us as your shining dwellings.

By your first coming, make us righteous;
at your second coming, set us free:
so that, when the world is filled with light
and you judge all things,
we may be clad in spotless robes
and follow in your steps, O King,
into the heavenly hall.

This 'Sequence' (see notes) was sung in most churches in medieval
England on the first Sunday in Advent. It dates from about 900.

## Advent

We pray you, O God,
graciously to cleanse our souls
and our consciences,
that as Christ comes to our hearts
he may find them made ready for himself.

There are two 'comings' of Christ in the drama of the Eucharist: his coming in the consecration of the bread and wine (with its sequel the Communion) and, earlier in the service, his coming to the heart and mind of the believer in the words of the Gospel. It is this coming in the ministry of the word that is referred to in this tenth-century French Sequence, sung immediately before the Gospel.

## Christmas

Lo, from a maiden's womb is born Emmanuel,
King of eternal years.
God, great and mighty, living here among us,
promised by prophets of old.

May he grant us all those joys
which he shares with his Father
in the heavenly Kingdom.

Glory, grace and victory,
through the ages of eternity
be to him for ever.

Using very few words, this ninth-century author's prayer-poem
presents to us the central mystery of Christmas — Emmanuel, God-
with-us — and asks for a share in all the blessings which flow from
the Incarnation.

## Christmas

A dry rod lacking moisture's dew,
in a manner strange and new,
bears both fruit and flowers too,
    like the maiden-mother chaste.

This fruit is her blessed child,
fruit of gladness undefiled;
Adam had not been beguiled
    if this fruit he'd chanced to taste.

Gracious Saviour of all lands,
held in Mary's loving hands,
though your throne in heaven stands
    in a stable here you rest.

Through this child to us now given,
may our sins be all forgiven;
help us, who on earth have striven
    and by perils are oppressed.

This twelfth-century poet likens the birth of Christ to the miraculous blossom and fruit brought forth by Aaron's rod (Numbers 17.8) and contrasts the life-giving fruit of Mary's womb with the fatal fruit taken by Adam in Genesis 3.6.

## The Circumcision of Christ

As we celebrate today the circumcision of Jesus Christ
and the octave of his nativity,
we adore with reverence your wonders, Lord;
because she who gave birth is both mother and virgin,
and he who was born is both infant and God.
Uniquely in time the heavens spoke out
and the angels gave thanks;
the shepherds rejoiced
and the wise men were summoned;
kings of the earth were troubled
and little children crowned with a glorious passion.

In this Preface from the Mass of the Circumcision, the Anglo-Saxon
author gathers together some of the themes of the Christmas story:
the joy of the angels and the shepherds, the visit of the wise men and
the martyrdom of the holy innocents.

## *Epiphany*

We give you thanks, O Lord,
because you have made known your mercy to the nations
and have declared your salvation to all peoples.
By your choice a star shone forth on this day,
brighter than all other stars,
stirring up the wise men
and leading them from distant lands
to adore the true king in his infancy.
By the rays of its light
it revealed the Lord of heaven and earth
born in our humanity.

The image of the Epiphany star has often led Christians to thank
God for the people in their lives who have been like stars to them,
brightening their lives and leading them to experience God's all-
embracing love.

## Ash Wednesday

Be present with us, Lord,
as we make our prayers,
and do not let your tender mercy
be far from your servants.
Heal their wounds,
and forgive their faults,
so that no sins may separate them from you,
and they may always be able to stay close to you,
O Lord.

On the first day of Lent, this prayer was said in English cathedrals by
the bishop at the blessing of ashes (a symbol of penitence and sorrow
for sin) just before he gave absolution (the assurance of God's forgiveness). With remarkable insight, the author sees the connection
between forgiveness and the healing of inner hurts, which makes
fresh growth possible. 'Lent' was the old English word for 'Spring',
so-called from the lengthening of the days, and it was often seen as a
springtime of the soul, a time for new growth and flourishing. The
prayer suggests that this happens by our staying close to God in all
our imperfection.

## Passiontide: the cross

A ladder stretches up on high,
by which sinners, doomed to die,
to the King of Heaven are drawn.

Reaching to earth's furthest places,
on the cross God's love embraces
all his creatures once forlorn.

Cross of Christ, by which we gain
health and victory through love's pain;
earth's green trees could not contain
such a precious fruit and flower.

Medicine for all that ails us,
healing when disease assails us;
when our human striving fails us,
save us by your mighty power.

The meditation of this twelfth-century poet (possibly HUGH OF
ORLÉANS) begins with the upright part of the cross, recalling
Jacob's ladder uniting earth with heaven (Genesis 28.12) and Jesus's
promise that, lifted up, he would draw all people to himself (John
12.32). In the second verse the attention moves to the cross's hori-
zontal beam, suggesting the reaching out of God's love to embrace
all his creation.

## The light of the cross

Lord Jesus Christ,
for our redemption you were raised up on the wood
    of the cross,
so that the whole world, which lay in darkness,
might be filled with light;
we pray that you will always pour that light
    into our souls and bodies,
so that by it we may come to the light everlasting.

While Hugh of Orléans saw the cross as a ladder (p. 30), this author's imagination pictures the crucified Christ as a beacon, or as a lantern raised up on a pole, which sheds its light to guide our steps through the darkness. The divine love which shines out from the cross will shine on us in its fullness at end of our journey. Perhaps in the author's mind were the words of Jesus: 'I am the light of the world; whoever follows me will not walk in darkness, but will have the light of life' (John 8.12).

## Passiontide: Christ's wounds

Lord Jesus Christ,
Son of the living God,
who came down to earth
from the bosom of your Father in heaven,
on the wood of the cross
you sustained five wounds,
pouring out your precious blood
for the forgiveness of our sins;
we humbly pray that at the day of judgement
we may be worthy to be placed at your right hand,
and may hear you say,
'Come, you whom my Father has blessed';
for you live and reign with the Father and the Holy
    Spirit,
one God for ever and ever.

The five wounds formed a favourite subject for meditation in the
later Middle Ages. The way they were usually counted was: the
head (wounded by the crown of thorns), the right hand, the left
hand, the feet (nailed to the cross), and the side (pierced by the
soldier's spear).

## Meditation on the last words

How, my Jesus, could you bear
such suffering to sustain,
racked with thirst upon the cross,
yet silent to remain?
Could it be, beneath the weight
of such oppressing pain,
you thirsted still more deeply
our salvation to obtain?

Uttering your life's last words
while on the cross suspended,
into God the Father's hands
your spirit you commended;
with a mighty shout you died,
your final breath expended;
thus for all was life regained,
your saving work was ended.

I shun humility, and you
the way of pride forsake;
I transgress, my punishment
upon yourself you take.
I eat the fruit, and gall is given
to you, your thirst to slake;
I seek a life of quiet ease,
you suffer for my sake.

The poet is meditating on three of the 'Seven Last Words' of Jesus on
the cross: 'I thirst' (John 19.28); 'Father, into thy hands I commend
my spirit' (Luke 23.46) and 'It is finished' (John 19.30).

## Palm Sunday: At the blessing of flowers and branches

Almighty and eternal God,
flower of the world,
odour of sweetness
and source of new life;
all your words in the law and the prophets
you have fulfilled for us in the humility of your Son
our Lord Jesus Christ;
at your bidding the crowd went out to meet him
with devout praises as he came to Jerusalem.

Look favourably on your people
as they give you the worship they owe to you,
and bless with your power this your creation,
full of new life;
that, as once your people gladly showed you their
    heartfelt devotion,
so those who now celebrate this yearly festival
may with pure hearts give you worthy service
and sincerely praise his holy name.

May we abound in the fresh greenness of holy lives,
as pure and bright as these flowers,
so that, when the burden of our flesh has been laid aside,
we may be surrounded by the fragrance of good works,
and be worthy to meet your Son, our Lord Jesus Christ,
in the heavenly Jerusalem.

The people would then carry the branches in procession, singing St Theodulf's hymn 'All glory, laud and honour'. (The modern 'convenience' palm crosses seem a poor substitute for the colourful flowers and greenery of the medieval Palm Sunday!)

## Maundy Thursday: The Last Supper

Love makes you, O prince supreme,
share this heavenly banquet with your friends,
giving them in a wonderful way
your sacred body in a morsel of bread.

Love, knowing that we were under sentence of death
because of that fruit of old,
gives us yourself, fruit of a maiden's womb,
in form of bread, that all may live.

Love, O Jesus, makes you do marvellous things:
your own hands wash the disciples' feet,
leaving us an example,
and showing us the way to live justly.

Love, in all goodness and conquering might,
then bade you say to your friends:
'I long to eat this Passover with you
before the time of my sacrifice comes.'

Love commands, and sweetly you say:
'I shall drink no more of the fruit of the vine,
until I drink it with you in fullness
in my Father's heavenly kingdom.'

This is part of the 'Song of Love' by JOHN OF HOWDEN
(d.1275). In his writings there is an attractive confidence in God's
almighty love, such as we find in the next century in Julian of
Norwich.

## Good Friday

Walking alone, Lord, you go to your sacrifice,
victim of death, and our death's mighty conqueror.
What can we say to you, knowing our poverty,
you, who have freed us from sin and from slavery?

Ours are the sins, Lord, and we are the guilty ones,
you, in your innocence, take on our punishment;
grant that our spirits may share in your suffering,
may our compassion respond to your pardoning.

Three sacred days are the time of our sorrowing,
as we endure now the night of our heaviness,
until the morning restores to us joyfulness;
Christ, newly risen, brings gladness for tearfulness.

Grant us, O Lord, to take part in your suffering,
that we may share in your heavenly victory;
through these sad days living humbly and patiently,
may we at Eastertide see you smile graciously.

PETER ABELARD (1079–1142), the brilliant French philosopher
and teacher, is best known for his tragic love affair with his pupil
Héloïse. After she became a nun, Abelard sent her a radically new
collection of liturgical hymns for use in her convent, of which this is
the Good Friday one. His hymn for Saturdays is well known as 'O
what their joy and their glory must be'. The quality of his poetry
suggests that even 'unsuitable attachments' can, through grace, lead
to fruits of lasting value and may reflect the many-faceted love of
God. Héloïse's love was one of the factors which made the older
Abelard much less arrogant than he was in youth, as well as provid-
ing the impetus for verses which celebrate memorably the love of
God.

## Good Friday: Mary at the cross

Mother of the Crucified,
standing with him as he died,
that which Simeon prophesied
pierced your spirit in that hour.

Virgin mother of Messiah,
virtue's bloom with grace afire,
as foretold by Jeremiah,
Rose that mourns the Lily-flower.

Christ, who followed suffering's way,
grant that on the judgement day
with your blessed saints we may
share eternal joy and light.

In your mercy, Lord, behold us,
may your mother's prayers uphold us
and your gracious love enfold us
in your heavenly palace bright.

This Sequence comes from a Mass-book once owned by the Fitton family, who lived in the lovely fifteenth-century Gawsworth Hall in Cheshire. The prophecy of Simeon that a sword should pierce Mary's soul is in Luke 2.35. The reference to Jeremiah is to Lamentations, where the figure of the mournful daughter of Sion came to be seen as a prefiguration of Mary at the cross. The rose is another Marian symbol, and the image of the crucified Christ as a lily is found in the church at Godshill on the Isle of Wight, where that flower is depicted entwined round a cross.

## Holy Saturday: the 'exultet'

Now let the angel-host of heaven rejoice;
let the divine mysteries rejoice
and the trumpet of salvation sound forth
the victory of the mighty King.

Let the earth be joyful,
as it is filled with the radiance of such splendour,
and the whole world know that it has escaped from
    darkness
and is bathed in the glory of the eternal King.

O the depth of your measureless love for us!
To redeem a slave, you gave up your son.
O necessary sin of Adam, which is also our sin,
and which was blotted out by the death of Christ.
O happy fault,
whose reward was to have so great a Redeemer.
O blessed night, which alone was worthy to know the
    time and the hour
when Christ rose again from the dead.

We pray you, Lord, that this candle, consecrated to the
    honour of your name,
may continue without fail to dispel the darkness of this
    night.
Accept it like a sweet fragrance,
and let it be mingled with the lights of heaven.
May the Morning Star find its flame alight,
that Morning Star which knows no setting,
and which, returning from among the dead,
shines brightly on the human race.

This chant, dating back to the seventh century, is sung by the dea-
con at the Easter Vigil as he stands beside the paschal candle, the
symbol of the risen Christ. As with John of Howden (p. 35), its bold
confidence in God's limitless love despite human sin recalls Mother
Julian's 'Sin is necessary, but all shall be well'.

## Easter morning

On the third day Judah's lion
carries back to holy Sion
spoils of victory from the tomb;
wakened by the Father's voice,
see his mighty Son rejoice
as he breaks death's gates of doom.

Death and life have fiercely striven,
to Life's Prince is victory given,
Christ the captives' bonds has riven,
many share his glorious reign.

Joy returns with this new morning,
night's tears vanish at its dawning;
life slays death, its power scorning,
gladness now has come again.

Christ the Victor, Christ the Way,
path that leads to endless day;
by your dying, death you slay;
grant that at your feast we may
at your table find a place.

Bread of Life, Vine, fresh and green,
stream that flows with life serene,
feed, refresh us, make us clean;
from eternal death's dread scene
guard and save us by your grace.

ADAM OF ST VICTOR (mid-twelfth century) was the greatest of
the Victorine school of Sequence-writers (see note to p. 26). He uses a
variety of images to illuminate the mystery of the risen Christ; those in
this extract are mostly drawn from St John's Gospel, e.g. bread of life,
true vine, living water. Adam's use of the lion as an image of resurrection seems to be influenced partly by Genesis 49.9 and partly by a
legend which appears in a medieval Bestiary, that lion cubs were born
dead and raised to life after three days by their father's breathing on them.

## Easter: Mary Magdalen in the garden

O Mary, do not weep, there is no need to seek any further;
truly the gardener and cultivator of souls is here.
Look within your spirit's garden for the husbandman of
    your soul.

Why this mourning and lamenting? Why is your heart
    bowed down?
Why do you gaze at the sepulchre? He whom you love is
    here!
You seek Jesus, and do not realize that you have already
    found him.

There is no need for sighing and weeping, for true joy is
    yours;
you do not know it, but consolation for your grief lies
    hidden within you;
you seek the remedy for your pain outside yourself, but
    you possess it within.

There is no wonder that you did not know the Master
    until he sowed the seed;
the seed, which is Christ's word, enlightens you:
he calls you 'Mary' and you answer him 'Rabboni'.

Washed in the fount of grace, you bathed the feet of Christ;
pour upon us the dew of that pardon which you received
    from him;
make us to share in that resurrection glory which you
    beheld.

Glory and honour to God, whose love prefers the sighs of
    Mary
to the Pharisee and his lavish feast.
He nourishes us with his grace, and offers to sinners the
    banquet of life.

The author, PHILIP THE CHANCELLOR (d.1236), was an extremely fierce church man. As Chancellor of the Church in Paris, he conducted a long-running dispute with the University, and even had a special prison constructed in which he incarcerated its scholars! Here, however, he appears as a tender mystical poet, meditating on the scene in the garden (John 20). He seems to suggest that external things are powerless to heal the pain of bereavement; in grief we need to draw on our own inner resources and find the presence of the risen Christ in our hearts. Mary Magdalen experienced the fulfilment of God's loving promise in Isaiah 43.1: 'Fear not, for I have redeemed you; I have called you by your name, and you are mine.' Philip, following tradition, identifies her with the woman in the Pharisee's house in Luke 7.37. She is a figure of hope, a sign that God's heart is delighted by passionate, penitent love.

## *Eastertide: the Good Shepherd*

Praise to you, O faithful God!

You never fail those who trust in you,
but you let them share your glory.

You fight for us against everything
that could attack us and do us harm.

You are our shepherd,
You free us from the snare.

You protect us who revere you, O God;
great is the sweetness that you give us.

This is a Sequence by NOTKER (c.840–912), a monk of St Gall in
what is now Switzerland. He was a much loved teacher who com-
bined humour with his learning and poetic gifts, describing himself
as 'the toothless little stammerer'. The Sequence is a meditation on
the theme of the Gospel for Easter 2, Jesus the Good Shepherd (John
10). The divine shepherd protects and feeds his flock and is their
liberator from whatever ensnares them.

## Ascension Day

May Christ grant this day to be a happy one
for all Christians who love him.

Christ Jesus, Son of God, joining
your divine nature to ours:
as eternal God you visited the earth,
as new man you seek the skies.

Angels and clouds attend you as you return to the Father.
And no wonder, since, while you were still a child,
a star and angels served you.

Today, Lord, you have given to those who dwell on earth
a new and sweet thing: the hope of heaven.
You are raised up, not as an apparition but as man,
above the starry regions, Lord of Kings.

What great gladness filled your apostles,
as you let them watch your ascension!

How joyfully the nine-fold angel hosts
run to meet you in the heavens,
as you bear on your shoulders the one flock,
that had long been scattered by wolves!

Graciously guard that flock, O Christ,
Good Shepherd.

NOTKER makes a satisfying poetic link between the heavenly
portents which attended Christ's entry into the world and those
that were there when he left it. His statement of what Christ gave
humankind at his ascension is tellingly simple: 'a new and sweet
thing: the hope of heaven'.

## Pentecost

Kind Consoler, come and teach
our poor spirits, fill our speech,
warm our hearts, for where you reach
nothing harmful finds a place.

Happiness, and pleasant things,
health that from contentment springs,
all the sweetness plenty brings,
come from your abundant grace.

Light that streams from every quarter,
seasoning each son and daughter,
you anoint baptismal water
with regenerating might.

Praise to you for your salvation,
making us a new creation;
we, by grace a holy nation,
once were children of the night.

Gift and Giver, grace abounds
through your gifts, our heart resounds
with your love that knows no bounds;
let our tongues their skilful sounds
in your praises now employ.

Author of all good, bestow
your forgiveness here below.
In your new life may we grow,
and, renewed in Christ, may know
all the fullness of your joy.

Despite the ravages of the Black Death, the fourteenth century in England witnessed a remarkable flowering of spirituality, seen in writers such as Julian of Norwich and Walter Hilton, who hold doctrine and devotion together in a healthy balance. This poem, probably written in York, combines warm devotional feeling with an affirmation of the goodness of creation and an awareness of the Spirit's activity in the sacraments and in our lives. See further, Martin Thornton, *English Spirituality* (SPCK 1963, reissued Cowley 1992).

*Pentecost*

Come, Holy Spirit,
fill the hearts of your faithful people,
and kindle in them the fire of your love.

Pour out your Holy Spirit upon us, Lord,
and cleanse our hearts;
make them fruitful
by the inward sprinkling of his dew.

These texts from the eucharistic liturgy for Pentecost week make
use of two contrasting biblical images of the Holy Spirit: fire (Acts
2.3) and water (John 7.37–39).

# Trinity Sunday

*At the beginning of Mass*

Blessed be the Holy Trinity
and undivided Unity:
we shall give thanks to him,
because he has dealt with us
according to his loving kindness.

*Before the Gospel*

We pray that after our death we may enjoy the high
    mansions
where burns the clear light, kindled from the constant
    flame
which is God, our vision and our eternal salvation:
the light which shines in the angels' hearts
as they fix their eyes on Christ alone.

*At the Offertory*

We pray you, Holy Trinity, our God,
to bless the gifts we offer
through the invocation of your holy name
and the power of your only Son:
that by them, with the Holy Spirit working in us,
we ourselves may finally become
an eternal gift to you;
for you live and reign in the perfection of the Trinity,
one God for ever and ever.

The light imagery in the Sequence before the Gospel comes from the
reading which precedes it, Revelation 4.1–10, with its description of
the lamps of fire burning before the throne of God.

## Trinity Sunday

Blessed be the Holy Trinity for ever,
one Godhead, equal in splendour.

O worshipful Trinity,
O adorable Unity!

By you, eternal truth, we are created,
By you, perfect love, we are redeemed.

Protect all your people,
save them and set them free,
rescue them and cleanse them.

We adore you, God almighty;
to you we make our song,
to you be praise and glory.

The author, writing somewhere on the fringes of Germany around
the year 900, sees that God's life-giving activity in creation and
redemption is all one.

## Feast of the Transfiguration (6 August)

Today, O God, you revealed your only Son
to the fathers of the old and new covenants
wonderfully transfigured in heavenly splendour;
grant to us, we pray,
that, as you have shown that your fatherly heart
delighted in him,
so, by lives pleasing to you,
we may come to gaze for ever on his glory.

In Matthew 17.1–9 the apostles Peter, James and John see Jesus
transfigured in heavenly glory. With him appear Moses and Elijah,
representing respectively the Law and the Prophets of the Old Testament. The Father's voice was heard saying 'This is my beloved Son,
in whom I am well pleased.' Because of our adoption as his sons and
daughters, the Father delights in us too, and promises us that same
glory.

## Holy Cross Day (14 September)

We praise you, eternal King, son of Mary,
whose cross is our salvation,
whose death is our life.

For us you became sacrifice and victim
on the altar of the cross.
By your death upon the cross
the gates of death are closed;
death is forever shut out.

The poisons of Leviathan are washed out by your blood.
Through you the sulphurous streams of Babylon are
    dried up.

To you, O Jesus, be glory and praise.

The sea-monster Leviathan makes various appearances in the Old
Testament: he is a playful creature in Psalm 104.26, but in Isaiah
27.1 and Psalm 74.14 he is a powerful figure of evil whom God
overcomes. Isaiah calls him a 'crooked serpent' and this tenth-
century poet seems to associate him with the poisonous serpents of
Numbers 21. Anyone bitten by them was healed by gazing at the
bronze serpent which Moses had lifted up on a pole: a prefiguration
of the healing power of the cross (John 3.14). In Psalm 137.1 the
waters of Babylon symbolize the sadness of exile; the poet's imagination makes them more sinister by giving them the sulphurous
qualities of the underworld rivers in classical mythology, so that
they become a powerful image of death. His playing with biblical
images and their associations conveys the healing brought to the
world by Christ's cross, and the strength of his victory over death
and evil.

# PERSONAL DEVOTION

Praise for earth and heaven — Our redemption
— God's mercy — Longing for God —
Guidance in doubt — Honest anger — Christ's
incarnation — The elusive Lover —
Christ's glory and humility — Love of Christ
— Fountain of mercy — Heavenly Jerusalem
— Our need of God — Christ the Good
Shepherd — Christ the High Priest —
Growing in Christ — Praising the Creator

*With you is the fountain of life;*
*in your light we see light.*

Psalm 36.9 (NIV)

## Praise for earth and heaven

Let all created things in their loveliness
give praise;
let the sun, moon and stars,
the night and the day,
the fields and the seas
praise the creative wisdom of God's all-providing hand,
whose glory and power gave them their being.

Let the melodious sounds of our cymbals sing praise
to the saving mercy of his divine and generous wisdom,
shining brightly before us.
It draws the company of faithful Christians
to seek the beautiful walls and gates of Sion,
which surpass the fair dwellings of Jacob.

There to his chosen ones
the Blessed Trinity reveals the radiance of his presence.
Perfect peace is there; glory and beauty flourish;
there is found the jewelled hall, the golden folk,
the fragrance of the lily and the deep red rose.

The heavenly Church cries 'Hosanna';
the cherubim and seraphim repeat 'thrice holy'
in eternal glory.
May God's manifold goodness join us to the happy
    company
of the redeemed, through him who saves all things.

From looking at God's love and beauty revealed in creation, the poet
is drawn on to contemplate the glories of heaven, using richly sen-
suous imagery.

## Our redemption

We pray you, Lord, look mercifully upon us,
and enlighten our hearts
with the splendour of your Son's incarnation and birth,
his passion, resurrection and ascension,
and the coming of the Holy Spirit;
that we may be strong enough to escape
the darkness of this world,
and, with him as our leader,
may come to our native land
of eternal glory.

This collect used at Mass sums up the saving events of the new
covenant: God's new relationship with us in the Son and the Spirit.

## God's mercy

Light and fountain of light, God most high,
                    have mercy on us;
in whose will all things are upheld for ever,
                    have mercy on us;
who alone are almighty,
                    have mercy on us.

Redeemer of all, and our salvation, graciously
                    have mercy on us;
Redeemed from eternal death by your cross, we
    implore you,
                    have mercy on us;
Word of the Father, sower of goodness, light of truth,
                    have mercy on us.

God the Holy Spirit, our Advocate,
                    have mercy on us;
Our medicine and our loving kindness,
                    have mercy on us;
God, Holy Trinity and Unity,
                    have mercy on us.

The nine-fold 'kyries' (from *Kyrie eleison*: Lord, have mercy) at Mass
were often addressed in threes to each Person of the Trinity.

## *God's mercy: the publican in the temple*

Standing afar off
was a man who had committed many crimes,
and his troubled mind was dwelling on his sins.

He would not raise his eyes towards the high starry heaven
but, beating his breast, he said these words, his face full
of tears:
'God, be merciful to me, a sinner,
and in your goodness wipe out my misdeeds.'

These words won for him pity and kindness
and he went to his house a righteous man.

Let us follow his holy example and say to God:
'Merciful God, be gentle with us and free us from sin,
in your kindness treat us as righteous.'

This is one of the earliest known Sequences, dating from about 850,
and based on Jesus's parable of the Pharisee and the publican (Luke
18.9–14). The poet's imagination brings the scene in the temple to
life by his skilful sketching-in of details, such as the tears on the
publican's face. He dares to call the penitent's example 'holy'; for
him holiness consists, not in being good, but in responding to the
undeserved goodness of God.

*Longing for God: Bede's soliloquy on Psalm 42*

As the thirsty deer runs to the springs of waters,
so my spirit burns for you, loving Creator,
and thirsts to gaze freely on you, the light of life.
Oh when will it come to me, that time of love
   for which I long,
when your face and your form are present
   to my sight?

THE VENERABLE BEDE (673–735) was a monk and teacher at Jarrow in Northumbria. He played a major part in keeping alight the flame of Christian faith and learning in the Anglo-Saxon Church at a time when it had been all but extinguished in much of Europe. His tomb is in the Galilee Chapel in Durham Cathedral, and more of his prayers can be found in Margaret Pawley, *Prayers for Pilgrims* (Triangle 1991).

## Guidance in doubt: Fulbert wonders if it is right to become a bishop

My maker, my life and salvation, and my sole confidence,
give me guidance, and the strength to follow in my life
    what I resolve in my prayer.
I am uncertain what to do, how I can best find
    peace of mind at the last.
For I am afraid that if I rashly accept the bishopric,
I shall do more harm than good to the flock that I am
    to care for,
so I think it best to leave the work to better men than I.
But then I reflect that I would not ascend the throne
    laden with wealth or with noble blood,
but rather as a poor man raised up from the mire.
And since this is typical of the way you act,
I conclude that all this comes from you.
So, unless you make it clear that you want me to,
I would not presume to change things.

ST FULBERT OF CHARTRES (*c.*975–1028) allows us to over-
hear as he spreads out his uncertainties before God and asks for
guidance. He compares his situation with the way God has typically
acted in the past: so often in biblical revelation God is a God of
surprises, who uses the most unlikely people to further his purposes
of love.

## Honest anger

Jesus Christ, righteous judge, Lord and King of Kings,
for ever reigning with the Father and the Holy Spirit,
now in your mercy graciously receive my prayers.

You came down from heaven into the virgin's womb,
where you took true flesh and visited this world,
redeeming your creation by shedding your own blood.

I pray you, my God, let your glorious passion
always protect me from every danger,
that I may be able to remain in your service.

May your power always be with me as my defence,
that my mind may not be troubled by my enemies'
    assaults,
and my body may not perish in their deceitful snares.

May your strong right hand which shattered the gates of
    hell
crush my enemies and their jealous schemes,
by which they seek to lay siege to the paths of my heart.

The tension of suppressed anger gradually builds up during this
prayer until it finally rises to the surface and boils over in the last
few lines. The writer is BERENGAR OF TOURS (999–1088) who
made many enemies in his dispute with Lanfranc, Archbishop of
Canterbury, over eucharistic doctrine. It may seem shocking to find
anger in a prayer, but it means that Berengar is being honest with
God about what he really feels: he trusts that God's love is big
enough to accept and embrace him just as he is. Spreading out nega-
tive feelings before God is a very healthy thing; there can be no
healing or progress if they're not acknowledged, and God can be
trusted to cope with them.

## Christ's incarnation: finding the lost coin

He who created all things in his wisdom
has helped us to regain what our primal foolishness lost:
our closeness to God,
lost to us by the serpent,
and restored to us by a woman.

Like the woman searching the house
with a brittle potsherd and a kindled lamp,
you appear in humility
to recover the lost coin
and restore the shining royal image in the human soul.

Let us then sing the song of the angels,
praising the King of glory and justice,
who sent to us his only Son,
that today he might free us from misery
and grant us the grace of his merciful love.

GUY OF BAZOCHES (*d.*1203) was a man of action; he was a hunting, hawking and fishing clergyman, a Canon of Châlons, who went on the second crusade in 1190. In contrast to this 'macho' lifestyle, his image of God's saving love in the Incarnation comes from the domestic world of Jesus's parable of the lost coin in Luke 15.8. We are the coin, and God is the woman on her hands and knees, patiently scraping away with a piece of broken pot among the dust and debris on the floor, searching for the coin. When she finds it, she wipes off the dust, and restores it to its former glory.

## The elusive Lover

Who is this knocking at the door,
shattering my night's dream?
He is calling me: 'O loveliest of girls,
sister, spouse, shining jewel,
quickly rise and open to me, sweetest one.

I am the Son of the Most High King,
the First and the Last,
who came from heaven to this dark world
to free imprisoned souls:
I suffered death and many pains.'

I quickly left my bed
and ran to the latch,
that the whole house might be open to my beloved,
and my soul gaze fully on him
whom it most desired to see.

But he had gone away
and was no longer at my door.
O wretched me! What was I to do?
Weeping, I followed the young man
whose hands had formed the human race.

The city watchmen found me,
and robbed me;
they took away my cloak and gave me another;
they sang to me a new song
which said I should be brought into the King's palace.

This strange dream-like poem is based on Song of Songs 5.2–8. The poet leaves us with the hope that, despite the ups and downs of our love-affair with God — he can often seem not to be there when we most want him — we are ultimately promised a happy reunion in the King's palace.

## Christ's glory and humility

How beautiful you are among your angels, Lord Jesus,
image of God, in the day of your eternity,
in the splendour of the saints!
Before the morning star begotten,
you are the glory and likeness of the Father's being,
and the undimmed brightness of eternal life.
How lovely you appear to me, my Lord,
in your divine beauty!

And yet, when you humbled yourself,
when your unfailing light divested itself of its natural
    radiance,
then your goodness beamed out to the wise men;
then your love shone out more fully;
then your grace shed its radiance more widely.

How brightly you have risen upon me,
O Star of Jacob;
with what radiance you have come forth,
O Flower of Jesse's root;
with what gladdening light you have come to visit me in
    the darkness,
O Dayspring from on high!

At Cîteaux, and later at Clairvaux, ST BERNARD (1090–1153) led
the Cistercian reform movement, which sought to return to a strict
primitive form of Benedictine monasticism. (Benedictines had
grown too soft for St Bernard!) Though severely ascetic in his lifestyle, he was warmly romantic in his devotional writing, especially
in his sermons on the Song of Songs, from which this extract comes.
To portray Christ's heavenly glory, he blends together imagery of
light from Psalm 110 and Hebrews 1.3. In the Incarnation, the light
is dimmed to suit our human eyes, so that we may perceive it and
reflect it in our lives.

## Love of Christ

Jesus, you are the glory of the angels,
you are a sweet song in my ear,
you are a wonderful taste of honey in my mouth,
you are the colour of heaven in my heart.

Yours is an abiding love,
for which I eagerly long;
to me, Jesus, you are the eternal
honey-sweet fruit of life.

Jesus, you are all kindness,
you make my heart wonderfully happy;
your goodness passes my understanding,
your love has me enthralled.

My most beloved Jesus,
hope of my longing spirit,
I seek you with devout tears,
I cry out to you in the depths of my soul.

Now I see what I have searched for,
now I have what I desire;
love for Jesus makes me languish,
and my heart is all on fire.

This is an extract from a long poem, parts of which are familiar as
the hymn 'Jesu, the very thought is sweet'. It is full of the tender
spirituality of St Bernard and draws on phrases from his writings. It
was probably composed by an English Cistercian at the end of the
twelfth century.

## The fountain of mercy

Let all who are unclean
run to the fountain of free forgiveness;
let no one despair of pardon
who seeks it with patience.

As an example for sinners,
the Son of God shows us Mary:
an object of derision,
full of seven demons.

Once no one was more base than she,
now scarce any is more holy;
she washed the feet of Christ
and anointed his head.

Christ shrinks from no one,
God does not spurn humankind;
let us give thanks to him,
with devout and flowing tears.

Those bare feet of the Lord
let us wipe with our hair;
from our abundant riches
let us serve the needs of the poor.

For MARBOD OF RENNES (1035–c.1123) the figure of Mary
Magdalen is an inspiration to Christians, who have received God's
merciful love, to go and share that love with others, and to give
loving service to Christ in the persons of the poor.

## The heavenly Jerusalem

May Sion receive me,
that peaceful city of David,
whose builder is the author of light,
whose gates are the wood of the cross,
whose keys are the words of Peter,
whose citizens are always joyful,
whose walls are the Living Stone,
its guardian, the King who spreads the feast.

The city is bathed in festal light,
eternal spring, perpetual peace;
its fragrance fills the heavens,
it resounds with joyful melody.
No strife is there, and no decay,
nothing is lacking or out of true,
since all are formed in Christ's own likeness.

O blessed heavenly city,
firmly founded on a rock,
our safe and happy haven,
I greet you from afar with yearning;
my desire and longing is for you.

HILDEBERT OF LAVARDIN (1056–1133) was Bishop of Le
Mans and wrote this poem of longing during a period of exile in
England, when he was being persecuted by William Rufus. Like the
Jewish captives in Babylon, he is sustained through the pain and
loneliness of exile by the vision of his true native land.

## Longing for heaven

Now my soul in its dryness thirsts for the fountain of
   eternal life,
my fettered spirit seeks to break free from the prison of
   the flesh,
it wanders yearning, like an exile, drawn to its fair
   homeland.

Who can tell the immensity of joy and peace that is
   there?
Houses rise up built of living pearls,
their high roofs sparkle, their dining-halls gleam with
   gold.

The buildings are held together by precious jewels,
the streets of the city are of pure gold like crystal;
mire and filth and pestilence are nowhere to be seen.

The meadows are green, corn springs up in the fields, the
   streams flow with honey;
colours distil their essence, spices fill the air with
   fragrance,
the trees are hung with fruit and flowers that never fall.

Christ, the reward of victorious warriors, I pray that,
when the warfare is ended and I put off my soldier's belt,
you will lead me into the company of those happy
   citizens.

PETER DAMIANI (1007–72), a rather morbid and ascetic Italian
hermit, here uses his vivid imagination to picture paradise both as a
cultivated rural landscape and as the holy city in Revelation 21.

## Our need of God

O King of heaven and earth,
you are rich in mercy.
I am poor and needy,
and you know what my deepest needs are;
you alone can help me and make me rich.
Help me, O God, and enrich the poverty of my spirit
out of the treasures of your goodness.

My Lord and my God!
I am your servant:
grant me understanding and awaken my love,
so that I may know and do your will.

You are the Lamb of God,
the Lamb without blemish, who takes away the sin of
　 the world;
take away from me whatever is harmful and displeasing
　 to you,
and give me whatever delights you and will lead to my
　 well-being.

You are my love and all my joy.
You are my God and my all.

This is a meditation on Jesus's saying in Matthew 5.3: 'Happy are
the poor in spirit' or 'How blest are those who know their need of
God.' Its last phrase, 'my God and my all', was a favourite of St
Francis of Assisi, who used to repeat it often in his prayer.

## Christ the Good Shepherd

You are the Good Shepherd,
you laid down your life for your sheep.
I am that sheep which was lost,
and yet you graciously feed me with your body and blood.
Take me up now, and carry me on your shoulders.
What good thing will you deny me,
since you have given me your very self?
Be my shepherd,
and I shall lack nothing
in the green pasture where you have placed me,
until you lead me to the pastures of eternal life.

For many Christians, meditation on the Bible is something they feel they ought to do but don't, because it seems to demand a level of concentration that is beyond them. They may have tried an Ignatian five-stage meditation, or sat for ten minutes with an open Bible and constantly wandering thoughts, and then given up the whole business amid feelings of guilt and inadequacy. The author of this prayer demonstrates a more relaxed and less daunting approach, which is simply to let the mind wander along the paths of free association, and see what fruit it gathers on the way. From Jesus's saying, 'I am the Good Shepherd' in John 10.11, he is led on to the parable of the lost sheep (Luke 15.3), and then to the familiar imagery of Psalm 23.

## *Christ the High Priest*

Lord Jesus, apostle and high priest of our faith,
though you were in the form of God,
you humbled yourself,
and wished to be like your brothers and sisters in all
  things,
so that you might be a merciful and faithful high priest
    before God,
and take away the people's sins.
Have compassion, we pray you, on our weaknesses;
by your blood, purge out from our minds the works of
  death,
that we may serve the living God.
Grant that we may come to the throne of grace
    with confidence;
may we obtain mercy,
and find grace to help us in time of need.

A prayer based on Hebrews 4.14–5.2.

## Growing in Christ

Lord Jesus Christ, Son of the living God,
grant that in my frailty and sinfulness
I may always keep your life and actions
clearly in my mind's eye.

Let me make progress in living like you
as far as I can,
so that I may grow up into your full humanity,
and become a holy temple in the Lord.

May your grace go before me,
and follow me,
and shine into my heart;
be my guide along all my ways;
let me be able to do all the things that give you pleasure,
and avoid everything that displeases you.

Direct my thoughts and words and actions
according to your commandments, O God most high,
that, doing your will in all things,
I may be preserved both here and in eternity.

A prayer of LUDOLF OF SAXONY, a fourteenth-century Ger-
man Carthusian, and a probable influence on Thomas à Kempis's
fifteenth-century *Imitation of Christ*. The process of becoming
more Christ-like involves a paradox: becoming more open to God
means becoming more fully and uniquely ourselves.

## *Praising the Creator*

The company of the angels and all humanity
praise the Lord of the earth and the highest heaven.
The high angelic powers and mortal men
rejoice and bless you.
All the creatures of the world adore you as their Lord;
the earth and the sea praise you and pray to you and
    love you.
The stars shining in the sky glorify the Lord;
all your creation gives glory to you, O King.
You sit above the stars at the right hand of the Father
    on high;
O King of heaven, have mercy on us your servants.

An unsophisticated Italian poet of the eleventh century reminds us
that, as human beings, we share the happy privilege of creaturehood
with the angels and with inanimate nature.

# THE
# SAINTS

Mary: conception, nativity, annunciation,
purification, assumption — Benedict — John
the Baptist — Mary Magdalen — Michael and
All Angels — Andrew — Stephen — John the
Apostle — Holy Innocents — All Saints —
Apostles — Martyrs

*Blessed are those who are invited to the
wedding supper of the Lamb.*
Revelation 19.9 (NIV)

## Conception of Mary (8 December)

O Eternal God,
it is right that on this feast of the Conception
of Blessed Mary ever-virgin we should praise, bless,
and proclaim you with joyful hearts.
For, by the overshadowing of the Holy Spirit,
she conceived your only-begotten Son,
and, with the glory of her maidenhood still remaining,
poured forth upon this world
the light eternal, Jesus Christ, our Lord.

This Preface of the Blessed Virgin Mary was probably composed by
POPE URBAN II in 1096. He makes effective use of the contrast
between light and shade, taking the idea of 'overshadowing' from
the annunciation story in Luke 1.26–38.

## Mary's nativity (8 September)

Garden where the south wind blows,
wafting fragrance from the rose,
where no man may entrance gain;

ground made wet with heavenly dew,
fleece of Gideon, moistened through
with the Godhead's gentle rain.

Hail, O glory of the sky,
shine upon us from on high,
pierce our darkness with your ray;

calm the sea, O star of ocean,
lest the tempest's wild commotion
overwhelm us on our way.

The enclosed garden (Song of Songs 4.12) and Gideon's fleece (Judges 6.36) are two of the many scriptural images applied by medieval poets and preachers to the mystery of Mary's virginal motherhood.

## The Annunciation (25 March)

The blossoming rose which is Mary
springs from the tainted stem of our first mother Eve:
she rises like the morning star amid the heavenly
    constellations,
fair as the moon.
Her fragrance surpasses every kind of balsam, spice or
    incense:
she is purple as the violet, dewy as the rose, white as the
    lily.
The divine offspring of the most high Father chose her,
that he might take his holy flesh from her pure virgin body.
Gabriel from on high brings her tidings of new joys:
the eternal King appears on earth;
and thus he greets his mother:
'Hail, Mary, gracious mother of my Lord, full of
    heavenly grace;
you, O blessed one, will give the King his earthly birth,
and become queen of the world.'
'But how can I become fruitful,' she said, 'who from my
    birth
have not known man, but remain a pure virgin?'
'Fear not,' replied the Angel; 'the Holy Spirit will come down
upon you in your chastity, and, made fruitful by him,
you will bear both God and man.'

O woman, truly holy and lovable,
from whom sprang our redemption,
the salvation of the world, and true life,

You are the Father's darling,
you are the gracious mother of Jesus,
you are the temple of the Holy Spirit.

The figure of Mary often brings out the warmth and tenderness in
Christian poets, as in this tenth-century French Sequence.

## The Purification (2 February)

Lord Jesus Christ,
on this day you were presented
by your parents in the temple,
appearing among men and women
in the substance of our flesh;
the venerable old man Simeon,
enlightened by the Holy Spirit,
recognized you, took you in his arms,
and blessed you;
graciously grant
that, illuminated and taught by the same Holy Spirit,
we may truly acknowledge you
and faithfully love you.

In York Minster, this collect was said while those taking part in the
Candlemas procession paused before the Lady altar. They would be
carrying lighted candles, symbols of him whom Simeon called 'the
light to lighten the Gentiles'. The story of the presentation of Christ
in the temple is in Luke 2.22–40.

## The Assumption (15 August)

Alleluia!
Blessed Virgin Mary,
you surpass all the heavenly companies of virgins.
Today, rejoicing, you run to meet Christ,
as you are exalted above the angels in glory,
radiant with shining light.

How blessed you are, Virgin Mary,
foremost among the daughters of Jerusalem,
surrounded by the songs of shining angels,
circled by honey-sweet flowers,
roses and lilies of the valley.

We pray to the Lord,
that with you we may share in his kingdom.

An eleventh-century Italian writer conceives of Mary's entry into heaven in a delightfully fresh and lively way with the picture of her running to meet Christ.

## St Benedict (21 March)

Let our choir sing to you, O Christ, with sweet voices.

From the humble dust of the earth you choose precious
    jewels,
and set them in the splendid realms of angelic light.

They are the wonder of those high golden kingdoms;
and a source of sweet devotion to those on earth.

What a noble fortune you spent, O God,
on the altar of the cross,
so that your Godhead alone might possess
these beautiful precious gems,

whose purity is your loving kindness,
whose dignity is the glory of heaven.

Praise to you, O Christ our King;
grant us the crown of your merciful love.

This Sequence is a home-made production of the tenth-century
Benedictines of Winchester for the feast of their patron. It contains
the striking image of God spending all his riches on the cross in
order to buy the precious jewel of a human soul. Benedictines played
a vital part in preserving the Christian way of life amid all the
violence and instability that Europe suffered in the early Middle
Ages. In his *Rule*, St Benedict provided for a healthily balanced life
of prayer, study, manual work and hospitality.

## St John the Baptist (24 June)

The holy baptist,
the herald of Christ,

we celebrate today;
let us follow his manner of life,

that he may lead us
along the way which he proclaimed.

Holiest of men, friend of Jesus Christ,
we humbly pray that we may obtain those joys

promised, when Gabriel appeared to Zechariah,
to all those who devoutly celebrate your birth.

Through these festivals may we come to those eternal joys,
where the saints of God rejoice together in holy bliss.

You prepare the hearts of the faithful for God,
that he may find there nothing crooked or base.

May he always visit his faithful ones,
and be pleased to make their hearts his dwelling.

May he clothe us in the fleece of that Lamb,
whom your finger pointed out as the one
who takes away the world's sin.

May we be joined to the companies of angels,
and follow you, robed in white, through the shining
    doorway,
O John, friend of Christ.

NOTKER (see p. 42) refers to Gabriel's promise, 'Many shall rejoice at his birth' (Luke 1.14), and makes a bold adaptation of the Lamb of God image (John 1.29), conveying the warmth and security of God's love in terms of being clothed in the Lamb's fleece.

## St Mary Magdalen (22 July)

She embraces the Lord's feet,
she washes them with tears,
she wipes them with her hair.

Washing them,
wiping them,
she anoints them with ointment,
she circles them with kisses.

These are the banquets
in which you take delight,
O Wisdom of the Father;

born of a virgin,
you thought it not beneath you
to be touched by a sinner.

A Pharisee
invited you;
but that which Mary offered
satisfied you.

GOTTSCHALK (c.1010–98) was a monk of Limburg who became Provost of Aachen and court chaplain. He dedicated a book of Sequences, written in the style of Notker, to the Emperor Henry IV. It is interesting to compare Gottschalk's treatment of Mary Magdalen with that of Philip the Chancellor (p. 40). Both poets convey the fact that Christ was pleased, not with the cold legalism of the Pharisee, but with the warm, vulnerable passion of the Magdalen.

## St Michael and All Angels (29 September)

Rejoice for ever, you holy order of angels,
before the smiling face of God!

Through all eternity you feed
on his honey-sweet praise:

we join with your prayers, and entrust to God
the uncertain course of our life.

For though he reigns in highest heaven,
he looks with kindness upon the lowest places of earth.

NOTKER (see p. 42) meditates with simplicity on the two-fold
ministry of angels: adoring God and supporting humankind.

## St Andrew (30 November)

Through the cross, Andrew obtains
lasting joy and happiness.
Now, Andrew, you see your King,
you stand in his presence,
you adore him.
You breathe out an odour of sweetness,
the fragrance of divine love.
Noble saint,
be for us an inward sweetness,
that breathes the balm of heavenly life.

The reason why the sense of smell looms so large in this pre-twelfth-century Sequence is that the poet is elaborating on the Alleluia-verse sung just before it: it runs, 'The Lord loved Andrew as a sweet fragrance.'

## St Stephen (26 December)

O Stephen,
great ensign of the King of goodness,

the prayer you prayed for your enemies was heard,
and helped them.

By your prayers, O Stephen,
Paul, once a persecutor,
came to put his faith in Christ;

now he dances with you
in the Kingdom of heaven,
where no despoiler draws near.

May our prayers like yours
keep us always at peace with our God.
Now, wearing your crown,
you shine among the purpled martyrs.

In Acts 7.58 Paul (then called Saul) was among those who consented to Stephen's death by stoning, and involved himself as far as looking after the coats of those who threw the stones. In a delightful picture of the effects of God's reconciling love, NOTKER (see p. 42) here imagines Paul and Stephen dancing together in the heavenly kingdom.

## St John the Apostle (27 December)

John, pure and beloved
friend of Jesus Christ,

for love of him you left
your earthly father in the boat.

You renounced the soft breast of a wife
to follow the Messiah,
that, leaning on his breast,
you might drink from that sacred fountain.

You beheld on earth the glory
of the Son of God,
which is gazed on by the saints
in the life of heaven.

As Christ triumphed on the cross
he gave his mother to your care,
that, in your purity, you might
look after that pure virgin.

Racked by imprisonment and burning,
you rejoiced to bear Christ witness;
you raised the dead and conquered poison
in the mighty name of Jesus.
Hidden from others, the most high Father
revealed to you his Word.
May we at all times be as faithful as you,
John, Christ's beloved.

NOTKER (see p. 42) makes the usual identification of John the Apostle with the beloved disciple who leans on the Lord's breast at supper (John 13.23) and at the crucifixion is entrusted to Mary's care, as she is to his (John 19.26). His later legendary exploits come from a second-century work, the apocryphal *Acts of John*. Here he emerges unscathed from a cauldron of boiling oil; he is unharmed after drinking a poisoned cup, and raises to life two men who had drunk from it before him and died. John is often depicted holding a cup from which the venom is departing in the form of a snake. (See M.R. James, *The Apocryphal New Testament* (Oxford 1924).)

*The Holy Innocents (28 December)*

Praise to you, O Christ!
You regard as wisdom,
what seems to others foolishness:

you call as your servants
those of both sexes and all ages.

These new recruits, your tender soldiers,
slaughtered by the sword of Herod,
today proclaimed your praises:

though their tiny tongues could not form words,
yet they acknowledged you, O Christ,
by the pouring of their blood.

The martyrdom of the innocents in Matthew 2.16 reminds NOTKER (see p. 42) of Paul's saying in 1 Corinthians 1.25 about God's foolishness and weakness being wiser and stronger than human wisdom. God has a special preference for what the world counts as weak and despicable: the marginalized and oppressed matter to him very much. There is still a child within the most civilized of adults that is embarrassingly hungry for love, though its needs are often ignored or trampled on. Yet it is very precious to God, who can happily accept its continuing basic need for love, security, pleasure and value.

## All Saints (1 November)

Mighty Father,
be present with us,
inflame us with your love,
defend us from harm,
reach out your hand to us,
grant us your good things
and the prayers of all your saints.

Make us servants of God,
give us your sweetness,
enrich our lives
and, after our earthly labours,
open to us the flowery fields of heaven,
and unite us with heaven's citizens.

RICHARD ROLLE (c.1300–49) was a hermit who lived in a wood beside the nunnery of Hampole, near Doncaster in South Yorkshire. This prayer of his was incorporated in a late fourteenth-century rhymed Office in his honour; he was venerated as a saint at Hampole until the Reformation. His writings display a warm romantic devotion to Jesus, focused especially on the holy name. He had a close friendship with Margaret Kirkeby, a nun of Hampole, who lived for a time as an anchoress (see note to p. 30) in North Yorkshire. There is a touching story of how Richard healed her of an illness when she leaned out of her cell window and went to sleep on his shoulder.

## Apostles

These are the heavens where you dwell, O Christ,
in which your words thunder forth,
the lightning of your miracles flashes out,
the dew of your grace descends.

To these you have said, 'Pour down your dew, O heavens,
    from above,
and let the clouds rain justice;
let the earth open and bring forth the seed of righteousness.'

Quicken our earth, which you have sown
with the fertile seed of the apostles' words.
Through their words, let us lay hold of the Word of the
    Father;
make us bring forth fruit to you, Lord, with patience.

These are the heavens where you dwell, Angel of mighty
    counsel,
whom you call, not servants, but friends;
to whom you have made known
everything that you have heard from your Father.

Through their various ministries,
keep your gathered flock together
and unite it in the bond of peace;
may we all be one in you,
as you are one with the Father.

O King, dwelling in the heavens,
have mercy upon us.

GOTTSCHALK (see p. 82) identifies the apostles with the heavens because his Sequence follows the singing of part of Psalm 19 ('The heavens declare the glory of God') with its verse, applied to the apostles, 'Their sound is gone out into all lands, and their words unto the ends of the world.' He weaves an intricate tapestry of biblical images, drawn from Isaiah (45.8 and 55.10), the parable of the sower (Luke 8.15) and Christ's prayer in John 17.

## Martyrs

How shining and splendid are your gifts, O Lord,
which you give us for our eternal well-being!

Your glory shines radiantly in your saints, O God,
in the honour and noble victory of the martyrs.

The white-robed company follow you, bright with their
    abundant faith;
they scorned the wicked words of those with this
    world's power.

For you they sustained fierce beatings, chains and
    torments,
they were drained by cruel punishments.
They bore their holy witness to you, who were grounded
    deep within their hearts;
they were sustained by patience and constancy.

Endowed with your everlasting grace,
may we rejoice for ever with the martyrs in our bright
    fatherland.
O Christ, in your goodness,
grant to us the gracious heavenly realms of eternal life.

This tenth-century Winchester poet alludes to the passage in
Hebrews 11.33–39 about the tribulations endured by the martyrs,
who triumphed through their faith.

# INTERCESSION

Asking for the grace of love — Peace in the
Church — Reconciliation — For a bishop —
Relatives — Travellers — Blessing a house —
For a pregnant woman — The sick —
The dead

*Will not God bring about justice for his chosen ones
who cry out to him day and night?*

Luke 18.7 (NIV)

*Asking for the grace of love*

You have shown us, O God,
that all your commandments are summed up
in love for you and our neighbour;
mercifully grant to us this grace,
that, despite our many sins,
your love may abound in us —
that love which cleanses us from sin,
through Christ our Lord.

Most of the prayers in this section come from the votive Masses
commonly celebrated in medieval England. A votive Mass can be
said on any ordinary weekday in honour of a particular saint or
mystery of the faith (for example, the cross on Fridays, Mary on
Saturdays), or to pray for a special need or intention. The practice
goes back at least to the time of Alcuin in the late eighth century.

*For peace in the Church*

O God, the giver of peace
and lover of charity,
grant to your servants true peace
in accordance with your will;
that we may be delivered
from all the temptations
which press upon us.

*For reconciliation*

We ask you, Lord,
to set us free from all evil,
and graciously grant
that, as we seek your forgiveness for ourselves,
so we may be forgiving to others.

## For a bishop

Grant, O Lord, to your servant our bishop
that he may preach and practise
those things that are true and right;
may he build up the souls of those in his care
by the example of his good actions,
and receive the reward of his labours
from you, the Good Shepherd.

*For relatives*

O God, you have poured into the hearts of your faithful
    people
the gifts of your love
by the grace of the Holy Spirit;
grant to your servants and handmaids,
for whom we ask your mercy,
health of mind and of body;
that they may love you with all their strength,
and do whatever pleases you
with all the love of their hearts.

## For travellers

O God, you always show your mercy
to those who love you,
and, wherever they are,
you are never far from those who serve you;
guide the paths and the actions of your servants
in accordance with your will,
that, with you as their protector and leader,
they may advance without stumbling along the ways of
integrity.

## Blessing a house

Hear us, holy Lord, almighty Father, eternal God,
and graciously send your holy angel from heaven
to guard, cherish, protect, visit and defend
all who live in this house,
through Christ our Lord.

This prayer was also used in church during the *Asperges* ceremony
before the principal Mass on Sundays, when the people were sprink-
led with holy water to remind them of their baptism.

*For a pregnant woman*

Be present as we pray to you, almighty God,
and grant to your handmaid
the gift of your generous protection,
that, when the time comes for her to give birth,
she may receive the help of your favourable kindness,
and that her child, washed in the saving waters of
    baptism,
may prosper happily and grow in grace.

## *For the sick*

Each passing moment of our life
is held within your will, O God;
receive our prayers for your servant,
for whom we ask your mercy in his sickness.

We bring to you our anxieties
about the danger he is in;
may we rejoice in his healing,
through Christ our Lord.

Unlike some prayers for healing, this does not attempt to browbeat
God into action, or try to be a spell for a magic cure; it brings to God
concern for the sick person within the context of a trust in his will
for our ultimate well-being.

## For the sick

You always govern your creatures, O God,
with loving kindness;
bend your ear to our prayers,
and look favourably upon your servant,
who is now bearing bodily sickness.
Visit him with your salvation,
and grant him the medicine
of your heavenly grace,
through Christ our Lord.

## For the dead

O gracious God,
you have called all people to share your eternal glory;
Good Shepherd,
you have brought the lost sheep back to the fold
on your kindly shoulders;
Righteous Judge,
when you come in judgement,
deliver from death the souls you have redeemed;
do not abandon them at the last.

Remember, O Lord, your servants and handmaids,
who have gone before us, marked with the sign of faith,
and who rest in the sleep of peace.
To them, O Lord, and to all who rest in Christ,
we ask you to grant a place of refreshment, light and peace,
through the same Christ our Lord.

*For the dead*

Release, O Lord, the souls of your servants
from every bond of sin;
raise them up among your saints and chosen ones,
that they may live in the glory of the resurrection.

Let light eternal shine upon them, O Lord;
with your saints for evermore,
for you are gracious.

# Notes

*Numbers referred to here are page numbers.*

3. Text: *Ecce iam noctis* in various versions of the Roman Breviary, e.g. the Dominican *Breviarium iuxta ritum Sacrae Ordinis Praedicatorum* (Malines 1865) Vol. I p. 20.

   This is one of the hymns which used to be attributed to St Gregory the Great but the evidence for his authorship is very doubtful. In the cathedral and monastery schools of the Middle Ages students learned to write Latin using the works of classical authors as models. This led to the writing of Christian poems and hymns in the metrical forms of the ancient pagan poets; in this case the metre is that of the Sapphic ode, a form with an interesting pre-Christian history which Sappho used for her Lesbian love poems. The form continued to be attractive to Christian poets but they used it to celebrate that love which, as Dante says at the end of the *Divine Comedy*, 'moves the sun and all the other stars'.

4. *Benedictus et superexaltatus* in *Prime and Hours* (Mowbray 1961) p. 249.

5. *In hac hora* in *Dominican Breviary* I p. 26.

   The full cycle of offices in the Middle Ages consisted of the 'Greater Hours': Matins (during the night), Lauds (in the morning) and Vespers (in the evening) and the 'Lesser Hours': Prime, Terce, Sext and None (at the first, third, sixth and ninth hours) with Compline as a final devotion before going to bed.

6. *Veni, Domine* and *Excita* in *Dominican Breviary* I p. 124.

These texts were originally part of the office of Vespers on the first Saturday in Advent. The first is an antiphon to the *Magnificat*. Antiphons are verses sung or recited before and after each psalm or canticle in the office. They either highlight a particular element in the psalm's message, or else embroider it with material appropriate to the season of the Church's year or the feast being celebrated. The second text is the concluding prayer from the same office.

7. *Domine Jesu* in the *York Missal* ed. W.G. Henderson (Surtees Society 59, 1874) Vol. I, p. 256.

This fifteenth-century text is the post-Communion prayer from the Mass of the Five Wounds, but it could well have been written originally for the midday office of Sext.

8. *Deus creator omnium* in *Oxford Book of Medieval Latin Verse* ed. F.J.E. Raby (Oxford 1959) p. 11, stanzas 1, 2, 5 and 8 (but reading *luctusque* for *luxusque* in line 8).

St Augustine tells us (*Confessions* ix. 7) that the Christians in Milan kept all-night vigils in church to

protect their bishop Ambrose from the threats of the
Arian Empress Justina. Borrowing a custom prevalent
in the eastern churches, Ambrose wrote hymns for
them to sing, to keep their spirits up during these
long watches. Thus hymn-singing entered western
Christianity. The Ambrosian metre (iambic dimeter)
became the norm for hymns sung at the offices, and,
as the Middle Ages went on, the classical rules for
verse-composition based on 'quantity' (which Ambrose used) gave place to rhythm and rhyme.

9. *Da mihi super omnia* in *Prime and Hours* p. 250.

10. *Salva nos* and *Visita, quaesumus* in *Dominican Breviary* I p. 114.
The antiphon to the canticle *Nunc dimittis* and the
concluding prayer from Compline.

11. *Qui placido* in F.J.E. Raby, *A History of Christian-
Latin Poetry* (Oxford 1953), p. 161.
Alcuin was a major figure of the Carolingian Renaissance, that revival of Christian culture in Europe
which took place under the Emperor Charlemagne in
the late eighth and early ninth centuries. The emperor persuaded Alcuin to leave his cathedral school
at York and come to Aachen to enrich the court with
his English learning. There he helped with Charlemagne's programme of reform and education for the
Frankish clergy and was active in the attempt to
impose the Roman liturgy on the churches of the

empire, in place of the local Gallican rite. Perhaps his best known prayer is the 'Collect for Purity' ('O God, unto whom all hearts be open') which Cranmer translated and put in the Communion Service in the *Book of Common Prayer*.

15. The final section *O mitissime Deus* of *Oratio S. Thomae Aquinatis* in editions of the *Roman Missal* and in *Prime and Hours* p. 237.

    When the feast of Corpus Christi was extended to the universal Church in 1264, the Pope asked Thomas Aquinas to compose the liturgical texts. The result was a masterpiece of medieval poetry. The Sequence for the Mass, *Lauda Sion*, and the office hymns *Pange Lingua* and *Verbum supernum* are well-known in translation: see *English Hymnal* nos. 317, 326 and 330 (*Hymns Ancient and Modern Revised* nos. 622, 383 and 384).

16. *Deus pater* in *The Sarum Missal* ed. J.W. Legg (Oxford 1916) p. 226.

    The Sarum rite was the way of conducting services in Salisbury Cathedral but in practice it was followed by the majority of churches in medieval England. As time went on it tended to replace other local uses, for instance that of St Paul's Cathedral, London, in 1414. A few centres, notably York, Hereford and Lincoln, retained their customs until the Reformation but all of them (including Sarum) used what was in essence the Roman rite with relatively minor local variations.

From the ninth century onwards in northern Europe Communion devotions like this one began to be incorporated into the liturgy. This Franco-German prayer style was more emotional and effusive than the controlled brevity of the Roman collects (for example see p. 4). Many have thought that the combination of these contrasting styles was an important factor in making the medieval western liturgy such an aesthetically satisfying medium for worship. See, for example, Edmund Bishop's classic essay 'The Genius of the Roman Rite' in his *Liturgica Historica* (Oxford 1918).

17. *Adoro te devote* stanzas 1–4 and 7 in *Oxford Book* p. 403.
For Bishop Woodford's translation of stanzas 1, 5, 6 and 7 ('Thee we adore') see *English Hymnal* 331 (*Hymns Ancient and Modern Revised* 385).

18. *O sacrum convivium*, the antiphon to *Magnificat* at Second Vespers of Corpus Christi, in *Dominican Breviary* II p. 120.
*Fac nos, quaesumus*, the post-Communion prayer for Mass of the same feast, in *York Missal* I p. 217. See note to page 15.

19. Part of *Transfige* in the 'Thanksgiving after Mass' in the *Roman Missal* and in *Prime and Hours* p. 246.

20. *Suscipe, Domine* in *Prime and Hours* p. 247.

23. *Salus aeterna* in *York Missal* I p. 1.

One of the artistic fruits of the Carolingian Renaissance (see note to p. 11) was the composition of Sequences, a form in which the liturgy gave full scope for creativity. Sequences are prose-poems (after the eleventh century they show controlled rhythmic patterning and rhyme) which were attached to the Alleluia-chant sung at Mass between the Epistle and Gospel. On Sundays and feast-days long complex melodies were sung to the final 'a' vowel of the Alleluia and words were fitted to these. The Sequence elaborated ideas found in the biblical readings, adding interpretation in lyrical form. At first only parts of the melody were treated like this, but by the mid-ninth century whole melodies were being given sets of words. In some monasteries boys from the song school would repeat a musical phrase that had been sung by the choir monks, or a similar effect would be produced by one side of the choir answering the other. This led to the characteristic structure of the Sequence: a series of double versicles where each versicle has roughly the same number of syllables as its twin because it would be sung to the same notes. (Where possible, e.g. on p. 25, the translation attempts to reproduce this feature of the early 'classical' Sequence.)

24. *Precamur nostras* in *York Missal* II p. 303 (among the appended Winchester Sequences.)

This is an example of the rather rare 'repetitionless' Sequence, an early French form of the genre, which lacks parallel versicles because the melody was sung straight through with no phrases repeated. This sort tended to be displaced by the more popular 'classical' variety (see previous note) but *Precamur* is found at Limoges and Winchester in the tenth century and it survived until at least the fourteenth century at Lincoln.

25. *Ecce puerpera* in Dom Anselm Hughes OSB, *Anglo-French Sequelae* (Plainsong and Medieval Music Society 1934, reprinted by Gregg Press, Farnborough 1966) p. 22.

This piece comes from the earliest phase of Sequence-writing (see note to p. 23): only two repeated sections of an eleven-phrase melody have been given words, so it probably dates from the early 800s even though the oldest manuscript containing it is a mid-eleventh-century one from Cluny.

26. *Virga sicca*, part of the Sequence *Missus Gabriel* in *York Missal* II p. 206.

This is an example of the later 'regular' form of Sequence, which evolved late in the eleventh century. The verse-form is like that of a hymn, having a regular rhythm and rhyme (the metre was usually trochaic tetrameter). Unlike a hymn, however, the melody still changes (as in the 'classical' Sequence) after each pair of verses. This piece belongs to the twelfth-century Victorine school of Sequence-writing, associated with the Abbey of St Victor in

Paris. The Victorines delighted in finding symbols and prefigurations of the life of Christ in the Old Testament, sometimes using considerable ingenuity to do so. In England *Missus Gabriel* was usually sung at votive Masses of Our Lady in Advent but at Westminster Abbey it was set for the feast of the Annunciation.

27. *Hodie circumcisionis* from the eleventh-century *Leofric Missal*, MS579 in the Bodleian Library, Oxford.

28. *Quia notam fecisti* from the Preface for Epiphany I in the *Leofric Missal*.

29. *Adesto, Domine* in *York Missal* I p. 45.

30. *Haec est scala* and *O crux* from *Laudes crucis* in *York Missal* II p. 102.
    This Sequence for Holy Cross Day, written c.1110, rapidly became very popular throughout Europe. St Thomas Aquinas used its melody for his Corpus Christi Sequence *Lauda Sion*.

    The last two verses of this extract formed one of the five 'greetings of the cross', which anchorites and anchoresses used to say every morning, kneeling before their crucifix. Many medieval churches had their anchorhold, a room usually adjoining the chancel, with a window looking on to the altar, so the occupant could join in the worship, and a window on to the outside world where counsel could be given to those who sought it. This was the life lived by Julian of Norwich, author of *Revelations of Divine Love* — the first known book written by an Englishwoman, and whose importance is only now, after six centuries, being truly appreciated. Several anchorholds still survive, for example at Saxthorpe, Norfolk, and Staindrop, Co. Durham. A thirteenth-century handbook for anchoresses, *The Ancrene Riwle*, has been edited by Mary Salu with a preface by J.R.R. Tolkien (Burns and Oates 1955). It gives fascinating details about their life which, though enclosed, was not entirely solitary; as well as the converse at her 'window on the world', the anchoress was allowed to keep a servant and a cat.

31. *Domine Jesu*, the Secreta (Prayer over the Gifts) from the Mass of the Five Wounds in *York Missal* I p. 256.

32. *Domine Jesu*, the Collect from the Mass of the Five Wounds in *York Missal* I p. 253.

33. *Mi Jesu*, part of *Cenam cum discipulis* (fifteenth century), the Sequence for the same Mass in *York Missal* I p. 255.

34. *Omnipotens sempiterne* from the Pontifical of Anianus, Bishop of Bangor, 1268, in *York Missal* II p. 327.

35. *Amor facit* in *Oxford Book* p. 412.
    John was Prebendary of Howden Minster in what was
    the East Riding of Yorkshire and began the building
    of the now ruined chancel. He was also chaplain to
    Queen Eleanor and to her son Edward I. He was ver-
    sed both in the scientific writings of Roger Bacon and
    in the Cistercian tradition of affective devotion asso-
    ciated with St Bernard (see page 62) and Aelred of
    Rievaulx. In his turn he influenced the fourteenth-
    century English mystics, especially Richard Rolle (p.
    89). For more information see F.J.E. Raby, *A History
    of Christian-Latin Poetry*, pp. 389–95.

36. *Solus ad victimam* in *Oxford Book* p. 245.
    Abelard the poet was as boldly innovative as Abelard
    the theologian. This hymn, like the more famous *O
    quanta qualia*, is in dactylic tetrameter, a metre
    which he pioneered.

37. *Virgo compar*, part of *Plangat Syon* in the fifteenth-
    century Gawsworth Missal, MS Barlow 1, fo 434 in the
    Bodleian Library, Oxford. Also, not quite accurately
    reproduced, in G.M. Dreves and C. Blume, *Analecta
    Hymnica Medii Aevi*, (Leipzig 1902) Vol. 40, p. 33.
    This Sequence is set for the Mass of the Five Wounds;
    the only other manuscript which contains it was
    written for St Thomas's Church in Dublin. Normally
    the Sequence at this Mass was *Cenam cum discipulis*
    (see p. 33). Before being acquired by the Fitton family,
    the 'Gawsworth Missal' was the parish mass-book at

Tredington in Worcestershire. Some of the curiosities of *Plangat Syon* are discussed by R.W. Pfaff in *New Liturgical Feasts in Later Medieval England* (Oxford 1970), p. 89 and in my article 'La séquence "Plangat Syon"' in *Questions Liturgiques* 4 (Louvain 1973), p. 295.

38. Extracts from *Exultet* in *York Missal* I pp. 111–17.
People have sometimes been shocked by this optimism about sin and redemption.

39. *Sic de Juda* from *Zyma vetus* in *Oxford Book* p. 236.
Victorine Sequences often build up to a climax by adding extra lines to their closing stanzas. Thomas Aquinas imitates this feature in *Lauda Sion. Zyma vetus* was widely sung in England: on Easter Monday in the Sarum use, and on Easter Friday at York.

40. *O Maria, noli flere* in *Oxford Book* p. 380.
Philip wrote it as the office hymn for Lauds on St Mary Magdalen's feast-day. There is a verse translation in *English Hymnal*, no. 231, and a version in *Hymns Ancient and Modern Revised*, no. 556, which incorporates part of another hymn by Philip for the same feast.

42. *Laus tibi sit* in W. von den Steinen, *Notker der Dichter* (Bern 1948) I p. 46.
'Good Shepherd Sunday' is generally the second Sunday after Easter but at St Gall in Notker's time it was observed a week later.

43. *Christus hunc diem* in von den Steinen, *op. cit.* p. 52.
    This example shows a characteristic of many early
    Sequences: a separate first and last verse, sung to an
    unrepeated phrase of the melody, outside the normal
    scheme of syllabically parallel double versicles (see
    note to p. 23).

44. *Consolator alme* in *York Missal* I p. 159.
    This is the Sequence for the Friday in Whitsun week;
    it is not found outside the York use.

46. *Veni sancte*, p. 164, and *Sancti spiritus*, p. 162 in J.W.
    Legg, *The Sarum Missal*.
    The first text is the Alleluia-verse for Whit Tuesday,
    and the second is the Sunday post-Communion
    prayer. This is a typical example of the terse Roman
    prayer style (see note to p. 16): the Latin original uses
    only thirteen words to convey two aspects of the
    Spirit's activity — the living water which both
    cleanses and makes fruitful.

47. *Benedicta sit* (the 'Officium' or Introit), *Ultimaque*
    (from the Sequence *Benedicta sit beata*) and *Sancti-*
    *fica* (the 'Secreta') from the Mass of Trinity Sunday in
    *York Missal* I pp. 213–4. The Sequence was sung
    throughout England and France, making its earliest
    appearance in the tenth-century books from Limoges
    and Winchester. The other Mass-texts date back to
    the time of Alcuin (see note to p. 11) and may have
    been composed by him.

48. *Benedicta semper* from the St Gall Prosarium verses 1 and 15–20, in von den Steinen, *op. cit* I p. 134.

This was a widespread Trinity Sequence in German-speaking lands and was sung to a variant of the melody of *Benedicta sit beata* (p. 47).

49. *Deus, qui hodierna*, the collect for the Feast of the Transfiguration, in *York Missal* II p. 213.

In the eastern church this feast has been observed since the late fourth century but it was slow to catch on in the west. The collect is first found in the Spanish-Roman Vich Sacramentary, dating from 1038. In the twelfth century the Cluniac monastic reformer Peter the Venerable (d.1156) championed the feast, and it spread widely under his influence. (By the end of that century there were 36 Cluniac houses in England.) It was not until the fifteenth century, however, that the feast came to be included in non-monastic missals, often in an appendix together with other new feasts such as the Visitation and the Holy Name. For more details, see R.W. Pfaff, *New Liturgical Feasts in Later Medieval England* (Oxford, 1970).

50. *Laudamus te*, lines 1–7 and 13, from the Winchester Troper in *York Missal* II p. 316.

Though not found elsewhere, the poem's style is markedly different from native Winchester Sequences. It has the Germanic features of separate first and last verses and several lines which end in vowels other than 'a'. The lines of Anglo-French Sequences ended in 'a' in order to blend with the simultaneous singing by a cantor of the final extended 'a' of 'Alleluia'. Performance in Germany tended not to involve a soloist, but had choirs of men and boys answering each other antiphonally, with the first and last verses being sung 'full'. This is clearly illustrated by the closing verses of the 'Alleluiatic Sequence' from St Gall, *Cantemus cuncti*: 'And children's voices echo, answer making' (*English Hymnal* no. 494).

53. *Laudent condita*, a Sunday Sequence found only in the tenth-century Winchester Troper; printed in *York Missal* II p. 306.

The sound of medieval plainsong is commonly thought of as something highly ethereal and spiritualized. Some have conjectured that musical instruments may have been used to accompany it: as well as the cymbals that occur in this text, there are references to harps, trumpets and drums. We also learn from St Aethelwold's *Regularis Concordia* that Winchester had an organ in the 970s. Playing it was a three-man job: one monk worked the bellows, while two others were needed to thump with their fists on the broad heavy keys.

The poets of the Winchester school wrote in a self-consciously literary Latin, studded with Greek expressions. Their language can often sound inflated, but in this Sequence it is used to good effect.

54. *Corda nostra* in *York Missal* II p. 181.

55. *Lux et origo*, a Kyrie-trope in *York Missal* II p. 243.
Just as Sequences began from the practice of adding words to the notes of the Alleluia-chant, so Tropes were formed when the same thing happened to the other Mass-chants, whether fixed, like the Kyrie and Gloria ('Tropes to the Ordinary'), or variable, like the Introit and Gradual ('Tropes to the Proper'). Like Sequences, they were a fruit of the Carolingian Renaissance, but not such a lasting one; their popularity began to wane after the twelfth century.

They have a historical importance, however, in that the development of miracle plays (and hence of all modern European drama) can be traced back to a tenth-century Trope to the Introit for Easter Sunday ('Whom do you seek in the tomb?'), which formed the script for a little play enacted at the Easter sepulchre in many of Europe's larger churches.

That romantic medieval figure the troubadour, or wandering minstrel, may have derived his name from *tropator*, a trope-singer. There are many different theories about this. Bands of them would do the rounds of the monastic churches, bringing the latest compositions. The chant-book they would use at the High Mass might have in its margin an earthy and passionate love-song with which to entertain the novices after dinner!

56. *Stans a longe* in *Oxford Book* p. 114.
Its use was widespread in Europe throughout the

Middle Ages on the 11th Sunday after Trinity when its source-parable was the Gospel of the day. In the fourteenth century the monks of Whitby Abbey, showing some originality, were singing it on the feast of the ex-publican St Matthew.

57. *Cervus ut ad fontes* in F.J.E. Raby, *A History of Christian-Latin Poetry*, p. 149.
Bede also wrote commentaries on the Bible, a life of St Cuthbert, and the remarkably careful and accurate *Ecclesiastical History of the English People*.

58. *Mi factor* in Raby, *op. cit.* p. 259.
A sense of unworthiness is usually a healthy sign in one about to take up office in the Church, and so it proved in this case. Fulbert made an excellent bishop, and he had been an outstanding teacher in the cathedral school at Chartres. Berengar (see p. 59) was his pupil. Classical poets were studied alongside Christian authors (see note to page 3) and he was equally skilled in both quantitative and rhythmical verse. This honest and intimate prayer is written in polished classical hexameters, but Fulbert is best known for his Easter hymn *Chorus novae* ('Ye choirs of new Jerusalem'), which is rhythmical and rhymed.

59. *Juste judex* in Raby, *op. cit.* p. 264.
Berengar was a pupil of St Fulbert at the cathedral school at Chartres before teaching at Tours. He became Archdeacon of Angers and ended his life as a

hermit. In his doctrinal writings, disapproved of by the church authorities, he argued against an over-realistic conception of Christ's presence in the eucharistic elements.

60. *Qui cuncta condidit* in Raby, *op. cit.* p. 308.

61. *Quis est hic?* in *Oxford Book* p. 158.
This eleventh-century piece has sometimes been ascribed to St Peter Damiani (p. 66). The passionately erotic imagery of the Song of Songs inspired several great writers on the life of prayer, notably St Bernard in twelfth-century France (p. 62), Richard Rolle in fourteenth-century England (p. 89), and St John of the Cross in sixteenth-century Spain.

62. *Quam pulcher* from *Sermo 45.9 in Cant.* in Christine Mohrmann, *Études sur le latin des chrétiens* II (Rome 1961) p. 359.

63. *Jesus decus angelicum* from *Dulcis Jesus memoria* in *Oxford Book* p. 350.
Bernard's romantic devotion to Christ's humanity can be seen as part of a wider romantic movement in the twelfth century: courtly love became very fashionable at this time in European secular literature (see Peter Dronke, *The Medieval Lyric* (Hutchinson 1972)). One theory among many is that it was brought from the Arab world along the routes of traders and crusaders and filtered up through Provence from Mozarabic

Spain. Both the secular and the religious romantic set great store by the name of the beloved, hence the growth of devotion to the name of Jesus, which became a liturgical feast. Parts of *Dulcis Jesu memoria* were sung as its Sequence in the Sarum use: it later became known as the 'Rosy Sequence'.

64. *Omnes immundi* in Raby, *op. cit.* p. 276.
Marbod studied at Angers under a pupil of Fulbert of Chartres, and became Bishop of Rennes in Brittany in 1096. He wrote a popular book about the qualities of various gems and crystals, a genre which has recently reappeared in the New Age bookshops of today.

65. *Me receptet* in Raby, *op. cit.* p. 269.
Like Marbod, Hildebert was a product of the French cathedral schools and studied under Fulbert's pupil, Berengar.

66. *Ad perennis* in *Oxford Book* p. 187.

67. *O Rex caeli* in *Prime and Hours* p. 249.

68. *Tu es Pastor* in *Prime and Hours* p. 249.

69. *Domine Jesu* in *Prime and Hours* p. 262.

70. *Domine Jesu Christe* in *Prime and Hours* p. 286.

71. *Laudat in excelsis,* a Trope (see note to page 55) to the Gloria from the eleventh-century Monza Troper

(MS Verona 90) in Ritva Jacobsson (ed.), *Pax et Sapientia* (Stockholm 1986), p. 83.

75. *Aeterne Deus* in *York Missal* I p. 180.

76. *Florens hortus*, part of *Hodiernae lux diei*, in *Oxford Book* p. 162.
    This eleventh-century piece is one of the earliest of the 'regular' Sequences. Its use had become widespread in England by the fourteenth century. The 'Star of the Sea' image probably comes from the ninth-century hymn *Ave maris stella*, and may have been suggested by a play on the name of Mary: *maria* = 'seas'.

77. *A rea virga* (wrongly copied in some MSS as *Aurea*), in *York Missal* II p. 82.
    It was the normal Sequence in England and France for the Feast of the Annunciation.

78. *Domine Jesu* in *York Missal* II p. 18.

79. *Agmina virginum*, a troped Alleluia (see note to page 55) for the Assumption from a troper at Benevento, in Olof Marcusson, *Corpus Troporum II, Prosules de la Messe* (Stockholm 1976), p. 110.

80. *Cantent te*, from the Winchester Troper, in *York Missal* II p. 301.

81. *Sancti baptistae* in von den Steinen, *op. cit.* p. 60.
    A sign of its popularity in England is the fact that its

last line, *Amice Christi Johannes*, was used as the refrain in a fifteenth-century carol 'Pray for us the Prince of Peace', in R.T. Davies, *Medieval English Lyrics* (Faber 1963), p. 157. The John referred to, however, is the apostle, not the baptist.

82. *Pedes amplectitur* in Raby, *op. cit.* p. 225.
The Sequence from which this extract comes, *Laus tibi Christe, qui es Creator*, is not found in any of the Sarum books but it was sung in England at Canterbury, York and Durham.

83. *Angelorum ordo* in von den Steinen, *op. cit.* I p. 70.
This small-scale repetitionless Sequence (see note to p. 24) never achieved wide popularity, but it did find its way into the tenth-century Limoges repertoire.

84. *Et Andream*, part of *Sacrosancta hodiernae*, in *York Missal* II p. 3.
This Sequence was sung throughout England on St Andrew's Day, except at Winchester, London and Durham.

85. *O Stephane*, part of *Hanc concordi*, in von den Steinen, *op. cit.* p. 14.

86. *Johannes Jesu* in von den Steinen, *op. cit.* p. 16.
Unlike the previous piece, which is not known outside Germany, this Sequence was sung all over Europe.

88. *Laus tibi, Christe* in von den Steinen, *op. cit.* p. 18.
A Sequence confined to Germany and Italy.

89. *Potens Pater* in H.E. Allen, *English Writings of Richard Rolle* (Oxford 1931), p. viii.

90. *Hi sunt caeli*, part of *Caeli enarrant*, in *York Missal* II p. 200.
It was widely sung in Germany, but in England occurs only at Whitby and in three manuscript missals of the York use.

91. *O quam salubria*, part of *Arguta plectro* from the Winchester Troper in *York Missal* II p. 299.
This is another local Winchester product and is not found elsewhere (cf. p. 80).

95. *Deus, qui plenitudinem* in *York Missal* II p. 179.

96. *Deus, largitor, ibid.* p. 178.

97. *Libera nos, ibid.* p. 178.

98. *Concede, quaesumus, ibid.* p. 174.

99. *Deus, qui caritatis, ibid.* p. 168.

100. *Deus, qui diligentibus, ibid.* p. 179.

101. *Exaudi nos, ibid.* p. 196.

102. *Adesto supplicationibus, ibid.* p. 231.

103. *Deus, cuius nutibus, ibid.* p. 173.

104. *Deus, qui facturae*, in *Dominican Breviary* I, p. cv.

105. *O pie*, an antiphon added to the offertory chant at requiems on the anniversary of a person's death, in *York Missal* II p. 184.
*Memento*, from the Canon of the Mass, *ibid.* I p. 189.

106. *Absolve*, the 'secret' prayer, and *Lux aeterna*, the Communion antiphon from the Requiem Mass in *York Missal* II p. 184.

All Bible verses marked NIV are from the *New International Version*, copyright © 1973, 1978, 1984 by the International Bible Society. Published by Hodder & Stoughton.

Also published by

TRI/\NGLE

The PRAYING WITH series
A series of books making accessible the words of some
of the great characters and traditions of faith for use
by all Christians.
There are 14 titles in the series, including:

PRAYING WITH HIGHLAND CHRISTIANS
Introduction by Sally Magnusson

PRAYING WITH SAINT TERESA
Introduction by Elaine Storkey

PRAYING WITH THE ORTHODOX TRADITION
Preface by Kallistos Ware

PRAYING WITH THE ENGLISH HYMN WRITERS
Compiled and Introduced by Timothy Dudley-Smith

PRAYING WITH THE ENGLISH MYSTICS
Compiled and Introduced by Jenny Robertson

PRAYING WITH THE ENGLISH POETS
Compiled and Introduced by Ruth Etchells

PRAYING WITH THE MARTYRS
Preface by Madeleine L'Engle

PRAYING WITH JOHN DONNE AND
GEORGE HERBERT
Preface by Richard Harries

Other TRIANGLE Books:

PRAYERS FOR PILGRIMS
Compiled by Margaret Pawley
Foreword by David Adam

A unique collection of prayers from different places of pilgrimage in Britain and all over the world, as well as prayers about the Christian life as a pilgrim journey.

SEASONS OF THE SPIRIT
*Readings through the Christian year*
Selected and edited by George Every, Richard Harries, Kallistos Ware

A rich and varied selection of meditations, poems and prayers from the Anglican, Roman Catholic and Orthodox Christian traditions.

LOSING AND LIVING
*Thoughts on every kind of grieving*
by David Maldwyn Owen

A collection of prayers, readings and poetry about all kinds of grieving, from bereavement to losing your job.

Books
can be obtained from
all good bookshops.
In case of difficulty,
or for a complete list of our books,
contact: SPCK Mail Order
36 Steep Hill
Lincoln LN2 1LU
(tel: 0522 527 486)